S0-BNU-129

MARK ALLEN'S
TOTAL TRIATHLETE

"DISCARD"

"DISCARD"

MARK ALLEN'S
TOTAL TRIATHLETE

MARK ALLEN WITH BOB BABBITT

HARRISBURG HIGH SCHOOL
JOHN HARRIS CAMPUS
"DISCARD"

CB

CONTEMPORARY
BOOKS

CHICAGO · NEW YORK

Library of Congress Cataloging-in-Publication Data

Allen, Mark, 1958–
   [Total triathlete]
   Mark Allen's total triathlete / Mark Allen with Bob Babbitt.
      p.   cm.
   ISBN 0-8092-4589-2 (pbk.) : $10.95
    1. Triathlon-Training.   I. Babbitt, Bob.   II. Title.
  III. Title: Total triathlete.
  GV1060.7.A55   1988
  796.4'07—dc19   88-1833
                                  CIP

All quotes by David K. Reynolds are from his book *Playing Ball on Running Water*, New York: Quill Press, 1984.

Copyright © 1988 by Mark Allen and Bob Babbitt
All rights reserved
Published by Contemporary Books, Inc.
180 North Michigan Avenue, Chicago, Illinois 60601
Manufactured in the United States of America
Library of Congress Catalog Card Number: 88-1833
International Standard Book Number: 0-8092-4589-2

Published simultaneously in Canada by Beaverbooks, Ltd.
195 Allstate Parkway, Valleywood Business Park
Markham, Ontario L3R 4T8 Canada

This book is dedicated to the top men and women in the sport of triathlon. You've helped keep that flame inside of me burning strong.

CONTENTS

FOREWORD

Team sports—basketball and baseball, mostly—occupied my athletic interests during grade school, high school, and college, and I enjoyed them immensely. My basketball-playing days were over in my early thirties, and I went into college coaching. I turned to tennis, biking, and swimming to maintain fitness and for the relaxation and pleasure they provide.

Then, in the early 1980s, the triathlon exploded on the American sports scene. At the urging of a friend who, like me, was fascinated by the television coverage of the Ironman, I entered the Portland, Oregon, Triathlon, a part of the first U.S. Triathlon Series in 1982.

Having never before competed in a running or a swimming or a biking race, I began a rigorous three-month training program in preparation for the triathlon. I discovered that my physical condition, which I thought to be reasonably good, was totally inadequate for the triathlon. The cross-training I was doing put new demands on my stamina and strength and required changes in my food and liquid intakes. I switched to a diet high in complex carbohydrates and drank more water than ever before—as much as 16 glasses a day.

During that training program, my stamina and performance improved markedly, so that on race day I completed the event in reasonably good time with enough energy to kick the last quarter-mile for the 15-kilometer run and to recover quickly after the event. I felt great. I loved the competition and the accompanying feeling of well-being and accomplishment. I was hooked on the triathlon and haven't missed a year of competition since. Along with the enjoyment of the train-

9

ing and competition, the well-being that I felt helped me to better handle the stresses inherent in a professional coaching life.

I also made new friends. Some were from team sports as I had been, but many others had been specialists in one of the three triathlon activities. These athletes, already skilled in the run, swim, or bike, had a jump on the rest of the competitors because they could be out of the water early or could make up time on the bike or run. They also had the experience of competing in their specialty and knew how to handle changing conditions in a race. They usually were high finishers in their respective age groups.

I met a third group of triathletes who had neither played on sports teams nor performed in the individual specialties. These people found triathlons to be the perfect entry into a sporting world they previously had observed only from the outside. Many have become fine triath-letes, but most of them are just pleased to have discovered a life of fitness and competition they probably never would have found without the triathlon.

I have been privileged to come to know some of the top triathlon professionals. I have acquired great respect for these men and women, whose conditioning levels are the highest of any athletic group anywhere. Their training work load, which Mark Allen describes in this book, is enormous. They need amazing dedication and discipline to carry it out—and, man, do they ever compete! Always right to the edge—and frequently a little beyond.

Enjoy this book written by one of the top competitors ever. It will help you get in top shape mentally as well as physically, so that you, too, can either enter into or move ahead in the wonderful world of triathlon.

Jack Ramsay
Head Coach, Indiana Pacers

PREFACE

I've thought about writing a book for some time now. I've been involved with triathlons for the past six years, and learned quite a bit about training and racing from them. However, several people have beaten me to the punch on books about training and racing techniques and theories. Enough great information is already available on those subjects to keep me learning for years to come.

I've been intrigued by sports, all sports, since I was a kid. I've always enjoyed hearing an athlete talk about how sports has affected his or her life. It's not just the statistics and the results that are important. What we remember most are those emotional moments when the underdog won or the favorites fell short of that ultimate championship. Those strong feelings pop into my mind when I'm out training or racing. Sometimes I become the entire

U.S. hockey team that beat the USSR for the gold medal in 1980. My down moments seem to have company when I think of an ice skater who fell during her final performance.

What I do for a living is very different from most jobs. I swim, bike, and run. My training for triathlons may seem extreme, but it must be for me to excel at it. It's a constant test for me to balance five or six hours of daily training into the rest of what I would call a normal life.

We are all different, each of us excelling in different areas. It's other people's strengths that we look at and use to help keep us going during the tough times. When we admire someone, we take that part of them we need and incorporate it into our own lives.

No matter what level of interest you have in sports, whether it's a diversion or a passion, you'll see parts of yourself

in this book. Take the parts you can relate to and learn from, throw the rest
away, and enjoy the stories. Triathlons
showed me an inner strength I never knew I had. They have also humbled
me beyond belief and taught me about
my own athletic mortality. Have fun
with what you read, and above all re-
main your own best teacher.

ACKNOWLEDGMENTS

My thanks to Bob Babbitt for his patience in weeding through all my tapes. And to Jerrie Beard, Beth Hagman, and Susan Buntrock for their patience with Bob Babbitt. A special thanks to Charlie Graves for getting this whole project rolling.

Mark Allen

MARK ALLEN'S
TOTAL TRIATHLETE

THE PLAYERS

Before getting into this tale of psyching, training, and racing triathlons, let me introduce the triathletes who play a big part in this story. You may already know some of them as that historic assemblage that has dominated the sport: The Big Four.

Dave Scott

Six-time winner of the Ironman, Dave has been competing longer than any other top pro in the sport except Scott Tinley and Scott Molina. He's helped pave the way for the growth of the sport. With a reputation as a recluse, he lives in Davis, California, and is infamous for his love of training in extreme weather conditions. He says it makes him tough to train under the 100-degree sunny skies of California's Central Valley. He feels that training his way gets him ready for the Ironman, and there is no evidence to dispute that. Also known for his massive but healthy eating habits, Dave puts away more food than anyone else around.

Photo courtesy of Bud Light Ironman

Photo by Lois Schwartz

Scott Tinley
The "Rebel" has blond hair and a blond mustache, and is famous for his Southern California semi-carefree lifestyle and attitude, even though he is one of the most driven guys in the sport. He juggles his clothing business, his wife, his newborn child, and training. He gets more done in 24 hours than anyone else around; it would take someone else three days to do what he does in one. His training is pretty regimented, the same year-round. Scott, an Encinitas, California, resident, has mellowed through the years; his rabble-rousing days may finally be behind him.

Photo by Lois Schwartz

Scott Molina

Scott's the workhorse, the blue-collar worker of our sport, and in a sense, the golden success story. He married his wife, Stephanie, at 21, and had a child a year and a half later. They lived in Pittsburgh, California, in a small mobile home, barely making ends meet, Stephanie cutting hair and Scott working in a liquor store at night and training during the day. With an unlimited amount of talent, potential, and drive, Scott moved to Del Mar, California, in 1982 and won practically every race he entered between 1982 and 1986. The 1987 season was not his best: those hard, long years when he raced once or twice every weekend might have finally caught up to him. Known as "The Terminator," Scott now lives in Boulder, Colorado.

Mike Pigg

The new guy on the block is from Arcata, California. Involved in the sport for only three years, Mike has taught us the meaning of consistent, hard workouts. He moved to Colorado for two months in the summer of 1987 and trained with me almost daily. Pigg has a thirst for training that doesn't seem to quit. He goes from one workout to the next. If he's home for more than two hours and isn't eating or sleeping, he feels he's got to get out there and train some more. He's progressed tremendously over the last couple of years. He's now beaten all of the Big Four: early in 1987, he beat Tinley, Molina, and Dave Scott in different races. It took him until Hilton Head to knock me off. Mike is one of the guys who holds the future of the sport in his hands.

Photo courtesy of Bud Light USTS

Photo by Lois Schwartz

Photo by Lois Schwartz

George Hoover

One of my best friends, George is the son of Nancy Hoover, one of the co-founders of Team J David. He has no athletic background except as a surf rat growing up in Del Mar, California. George has more coordination and talent than anyone else in triathlons. He's been in the sport as long as I have, but he went through a lot of turmoil when J David went down the tubes. In 1986, he finished third in Nice, and in 1987 he was in really good shape when he crashed in Monterey. The fall put him out for the bulk of the summer. He ended the season with a ninth place in Ironman and a mechanical failure in Nice.

Julie Moss

The world became acquainted with triathlons when ABC aired Julie's emotional finish and near victory in 1982. I happened to be one of the millions glued to the TV choking back the tears as she struggled through what seemed to be an eternal moment. Three months later I owned my first racing bike and traded in my "moldy oldies" for a real pair of running shoes. Since that time, Julie has become my closest friend. She helps provide me with the balance and clear perspective I need in a sport that can easily become an overly obsessive and dominant force in my life.

Photo by Lois Schwartz

Ken Souza

Left: The best biathlete in the world, Ken is unbeatable in that sport when he's feeling good. He's trying to make the transition to triathlons, but swimming is his Achilles' heel. In the water, he's more like a piece of cement than a swan. He's definitely tough to train with when he's feeling good. When he feels like beating you up, you can't do a thing about it. Few people out there can go as hard for as long as he can. Souza lived in Boulder during the summer of 1987 and trained with Mike Pigg and me. When he's on, watch out.

Mark Allen

Right: "The Grip." That's me. I split my year between Boulder, Colorado, in the summer and Vista, California, in the winter; I'm into ideal weather year-round. I received the name "The Grip" a couple of years back. We had an infamous ride in San Diego every Wednesday: 90–100 miles along the coast to San Clemente and back, open to cyclists of all abilities. During those rides, I just loved to make people hurt. When they started to back off, I'd really try to hammer. When they'd go hard, I'd go harder. I'd start to hammer, and they'd try to hang on. After those rides, somebody warned another rider, "You've got to watch out when Mark gets down in the drops of his handlebars. He's got this death grip, and you've got to hold on for dear life."

I don't think I train any harder than anyone else . . . I just don't let 'em see me go easy.

Photo by Lois Schwartz

THE RACES

Here's a list of the triathlons I've competed in since I took up this crazy sport.

DNF = Did not finish
DQ = Disqualified

Name	Location	Place Finished
1982		
USTS San Diego	San Diego, CA	4
USTS Los Angeles	Los Angeles, CA	3
Horny Toad Triterium	San Diego, CA	1
Ironman Triathlon	Kona, HI	DNF
Malibu Triathlon	Malibu, CA	DNF
World Triathlon Championship	Nice, France	1
1983		
Gulf Coast Triathlon	Panama City, FL	2
USTS San Diego	San Diego, CA	5
King of the Hill Triathlon	Big Bear, CA	1
Ogden Triathlon	Ogden, UT	1
World Triathlon Championship	Nice, France	1
Ironman Triathlon	Kona, HI	3
1984		
Gulf Coast Triathlon	Panama City, FL	1
USTS Tampa Bay	Tampa Bay, FL	1
U.S. Olympian Triathlon	Las Vegas, NV	1
New York Crystal Lite Triathlon	New York, NY	1
World Triathlon Championship	Nice, France	1
Ironman Triathlon	Kona, HI	5
Cyprus Superstars	Cyprus	5

——— 1985 ———

Gulf Coast Triathlon	Panama City, FL	1
Avignon Triathlon	Avignon, France	2
President's Triathlon	Dallas, TX	1
Champion Auto Triathlon	Minneapolis, MN	2
Triathlon Do Guaruja	Santos, Brazil	1
USTS Chicago	Chicago, IL	2
USTS National Championship	Hilton Head, SC	3
World Triathlon Championship	Nice, France	1
Kauai Classic	Kauai, HI	1

——— 1986 ———

Grenoble Winter Triathlon	Grenoble, France	8
Great Race Triathlon	Queensland, Australia	1
Avignon Triathlon	Avignon, France	1
President's Triathlon	Dallas, TX	1
Wang International Triathlon	Toronto, ON, Canada	1
International Friendship Triathlon	Youngstown, OH	1
Nike Triterium	Oceanside, CA	2
USTS Chicago	Chicago, IL	DQ
Japan Ironman Triathlon	Lake Biwa, Japan	1
World Triathlon Championship	Nice, France	1
Ironman Triathlon	Kona, HI	2
Guatemala Triathlon	Tikal, Guatemala	2

——— 1987 ———

World Sprint Championship	Perth, Australia	5
President's Triathlon	Dallas, TX	1
Avignon Triathlon	Avignon, France	1
USTS Atlanta	Atlanta, GA	1
USTS Baltimore	Baltimore, MD	1
USTS Chicago	Chicago, IL	1
Vancouver International Triathlon	Vancouver, BC, Canada	1
Bermuda Triathlon	Hamilton, Bermuda	1
Music City Triathlon	Nashville, TN	1
USTS National Championship	Hilton Head, SC	2
Ironman Triathlon	Kona, HI	2
Guatemala Triathlon	Tikal, Guatemala	2

INTRODUCTION

Hold your goals. Fight your fight and live with purpose.

—David K. Reynolds

Recently, I spent the entire day in Fresno, California, looking at pistachio trees and fig trees and learning everything there is to know about grapes. Most people wouldn't think a professional triathlete would have anything to do with figs, except maybe to eat a few on a long training ride, but I've got to have a tax shelter, and figs seem as good a one as any.

The stress in my life is physical. The stress in the business world is emotional, but it can be just as demanding. When someone asks me, "How can you do triathlons? How can you do something that takes up to eight hours to complete?" I think about my day among the figs and wonder how anyone can spend a full day doing business and worrying about financial details.

Nowadays I need to learn to manage my money, handle taxes, and make investments so that the money I earn as an athlete doesn't disappear into the hands of the IRS. Otherwise, I could end up broke at the end of my career. But I don't know how people do business day after day. I think I'd rather ride my bike.

Like me, most people have short-term and long-term goals. Becoming a figologist and checking out tax shelters will help me reach one of my long-term goals, which is financial security. On the other hand, spending the day in Fresno kept me from training for a more short-term goal—my goal for the 1987 season, which was to win the Ironman Triathlon.

I had done the Ironman before, in 1982, 1983, 1984, and 1986. But until the fall of 1986, I didn't realize how important winning the Ironman was. And in 1987, for the first time, I felt I really had a chance to win.

For me, the summer consists mainly

This is me, Mark Allen, just trying to make a little splash in the world of triathlons.
Photo courtesy of All Sport Photography

of short-distance races, United States Triathlon Series (USTS) type events—a 1,500-yard swim, followed by a 25-mile bike ride, and then a 6.2 mile run. These are great distances to race every week, but the Ironman is a totally different animal—a 2.4 mile swim, a 112-mile bike ride, and a 26.2-mile run.

In September of 1986, I won the Nice triathlon—a 2-mile swim, 75-mile bike ride, and a 20-mile run—for the fifth time in October 1986. For some reason I didn't feel as fulfilled as I thought I would. I didn't feel I had stretched my capabilities to push beyond what I already knew I could do. I only had to put out maybe an 80–85 percent effort to do it, and there's a huge difference between going 85 percent and putting out 100 percent.

In the Nice race, you go as hard as you can go; when you start feeling you are going too fast, *that's* the pace you need to maintain. But in the Ironman, you have to hold back the entire day. You hold back maybe 5 to 10 percent during the swim and bike ride, but by the time you get to the marathon, you still feel pretty well spent. That's because the temperature is always 100 degrees, and there are still 26.2 miles to go.

So you run past the airport, past the yacht harbor, past the people still going in the other direction on their bikes, and you're still holding back. You turn around with 10 miles left, and you're still holding back. You get back to the airport, make it past the last little upgrade before you reach the town of Kona, then finally hit the last little downhill. Then you've finally made it—during those last 500 yards, it's OK to pick up the pace.

On the flight home from France in 1986, a good friend of mine, photographer Tracy Frankel, said, "You really ought to think about doing the Ironman. I know it's only two weeks away, and I know it's not much recovery time. But, hey, if you feel good . . . just go for it!"

So I entered on short notice and had a good day, breaking Scott Tinley's 1985 course record by 14 minutes. Unfortunately, Dave Scott broke the old record by 20 minutes, and I finished second, 6 minutes back.

As I stood on the stage during the awards ceremony the next evening, I watched and listened as Dave gave his acceptance speech. I felt the electricity in the air. I looked out at all the people and thought, "This is one heavy, heavy race. I really want to *win* this race." That's why in 1987 I decided to skip Nice and concentrate specifically on the Ironman. That year, I felt, "My time is *now.*"

For 1987 my focus had changed dramatically. I'd proved that I could win Nice, but could I win the Ironman? In 1986 there was no pressure on me at all, because when I arrived in Kona, there were absolutely no expectations. If I did poorly, everyone would say, "Well, what do you expect? The guy just won Nice two weeks ago!" If I did great, it would be a major surprise. It was a win-win situation.

In 1987, by making my goal to win the Ironman public knowledge, I put a lot of pressure on myself. Sometimes we need to do that in order to get better results. Every morning when I woke up, I'd remember my commitment and know I didn't have Nice to fall back on. If I had a great race in Hawaii, the reaction would be, "Well, he geared up for the race all year . . . he'd *better* have a good one." And if I did poorly, people would wonder if I'm really well suited for Hawaii's extreme conditions.

But if you don't put yourself on the line, if you don't take risks in life, why play the game? That's true not only in triathlons, but in everything we do. I had grown complacent winning Nice repeatedly, and I think by having Ironman as my end-of-the-season goal, I worked harder along the way to turn that goal into a reality.

I prepared for the short races like other people prepare for a business meeting or a test. The Ironman was my final exam. The weekly tune-ups, either in athletics or in business, teach you how hard you can push and how far you can go. If you perform poorly, you have a chance to redeem yourself the next week. The big deals, like Ironman, demand consistency, commitment, patience, and preparation. You invest in that goal every single day of the year. The mental and physical effort, the highs and the lows, are all seeds that you plant along the way. Race day is harvest time; that's when you reap the benefits.

What makes down-the-line events like the Ironman so difficult is that no matter how ready you are, you have to be able to deal with the unexpected. Your car might break down on the way to the final exam, or you might come down with the flu before a major presentation. That's what they call the luck of the draw. All you can do is prepare to the best of your ability and then roll the dice. Achieving that goal may come down to how well you deal with the adversity that comes your way.

No matter what profession you're in, goals test your mind, your body, and your soul. This book is a look at my whole career and, more specifically, my preparation for and participation in the 1987 Ironman. It was the biggest challenge of my life.

Right before my visit to the fig trees, my training for the Ironman had finally started to come together. I had begun training specifically for Ironman right after I won the Bermuda Triathlon on August 16, 1987. I increased my training miles and cut back on speed work. The long-distance training puts a different kind of stress on the body—oh, sure, you get sore from doing speed work because it's so intense, but it's just not the same. Every year when I start training for the Ironman, I realize I've forgotten how tired it makes me. It's hard to find a balance between doing the miles I think I need to do and absorbing the miles and improving.

But the day before my trip to Fresno, I finally felt I was starting to get used to the miles and to get a little bit more spring back in my legs. I could finally feel the speed I had before I started concentrating on the long training. For the first time in the season, I could taste the Ironman. Until then, I felt like my performance was going to fall short of

what it would take to beat Dave Scott. But on that day, I felt like I had it in me to win. I *knew* what I could do.

So it felt strange to be in Fresno looking at pistachio trees, talking about tax shelters and investments, and losing a day of Ironman training: no workouts, just work. It made me wonder what I was doing there. Just as I get momentum going, something always seems to come along to break it up. What's the right balance?

But that's part of the game. Every triathlete has to balance family life, business life, training life, racing life, and sponsorship life. Part of you has to say, "Am I doing what I want to do? Am I selling myself short? Am I selling myself out? Am I compromising what I want to do and be just to make a buck? Am I putting enough back into the sport?"

This book is all about that balance, not only for the beginning triathlete, but also for the seasoned athlete and the weekend warrior who wants to accomplish just a little more in his or her sport. Take what you can from my experiences and apply it to your own life. Make every challenge your own personal Ironman.

1
THE BEGINNING: "HEY, WHO ARE YOU?"

Life must be lived moment by moment. There are no golden hours, only ready people.
—David K. Reynolds

I saw the Ironman for the first time on TV in 1982, when Julie Moss fell and crawled across the finish line. Everyone in the room was all choked up. People were crying and cheering. I thought, "This is incredible." I'd heard of the Ironman, but that year a friend and fellow lifeguard, Reed Gregorson, had entered, so I had a special interest in watching. He finished fifth while Scott Tinley won for the first time.

I remember thinking, "I've done a few lifeguard competitions with Gregorson, and if he can get fifth, I can at least get in the top 50 or top 100." I decided right then that I wanted to try it.

I had run maybe two or three 10-K races in my life, maybe 100 miles total at the time. It wasn't like I had any background in running. Cycling was something I did as a kid, a necessity, a way to get to school and back. I thought, "OK, if I train for this and life-

guard, it's going to take up all my time. So I won't have to think about what I'm going to do for a career."

At the time, I was doing a lot of thinking about a career. Working in a lab was out. Bunny Stein, my girlfriend at the time, was working in a lab, and it seemed OK. But it was a dead-end deal unless you got your Ph.D., and that definitely didn't appeal to me. I thought about going into marine biology. But that meant always having to scramble for grants. You had to publish papers in order to build a reputation in order to get a grant so you could halfway do what you wanted to do. Does that sound like a negative attitude? I don't know; maybe it was, but maybe that's why it wouldn't have been the right thing for me to do.

I bought some running shoes and spent a thousand dollars on a bike. It was all the money I had saved, but I was ready to go. I talked to my dad and said, "Hey, I'm going to do this thing called the *Ironman*, a 2.4-mile swim, a 112-mile bike, and a 26.2-mile run." And he said, "Gee, that's great, Mark. Now, what are you going to do for a living?" Little did he know!

In the end, I became a triathlete for myself. I really wanted to do it just to do it. At first I said, "I don't care what he thinks or what anyone else thinks!" I wasn't planning to make any money, I just wanted to race. Because of that, it was easy for me to do the training that was required.

I was overwhelmed at first, realizing what I was going to have to do, starting from ground zero in running and cycling and getting myself to the point where I could complete a race like the Ironman. I had only seven months to get ready. But since I wasn't doing it for anyone but myself, and because I wasn't doing it for money, glory, or my dad, the sport came easy to me.

I picked people who were really good in the individual sports and trained with them. I didn't care if they destroyed me in workouts, just as long as I was learning. I seemed to progress fairly quickly. I bought my running shoes and bike in April, and trained through April and May while lifeguarding full-time.

I competed in my first race on June 12, 1982. It was the first-ever USTS San Diego event, a 2-kilometer swim, 30-kilometer bike, and 15-kilometer run. I was OK during the swim and did fine on the bike ride. When I got off the bike, someone ran up behind me—it was Scott Tinley.

He said, "Who are you?"

I looked at him running right alongside me and said, "Mark Allen."

"Oh, yeah, I've heard your name. Someone told me about you. Someone said to look out for you."

I was so excited. Here I was racing with Scott Tinley, who had just won the Ironman. I was doing great, running with Tinley, Molina, and Dale Basescu. They all pulled away after about two miles though. I couldn't hold on to the pace, so I thought, "What's it matter? I'm doing all right." I caught Dale Basescu, actually pulled away from him, and ended up fourth—behind Dave Scott (who obliterated everyone), Tinley, and Molina.

It was the first time in my life that I had ever come from behind like that, that I ever came back to pass somebody. In swimming, if someone pulled away from me, I always gave up. Already, something in this sport was different for me. That resistance wasn't there, and I wasn't afraid to really push it. I wasn't willing to give up, either.

My second race was the USTS Los Angeles in Long Beach on July 10. I finished third, behind Tinley and Molina. I probably would have been fourth again, but Dave Scott didn't enter.

My next race was the Horny Toad Triathlon, a 1.5-mile swim, a 56-mile bike, and a 13.1-mile run in August 1982. That's where I first beat Tinley and Molina.

A week before Horny Toad, I got sick. Usually when I get sick, I freak out, because my workouts aren't the same as when I'm healthy. This time I said, "OK, this is happening for a reason. You've got to look at why you're getting sick. Maybe you're too tired, maybe you need to rest—maybe you're a little nervous about the race and you're afraid of doing badly."

I just listened to my body and did

what workouts I could do, and by race day, my attitude was pretty good. I got off the bike with a 30-second lead, and I couldn't believe I was first. I kept thinking, "I'm going to run as hard as I can until they catch me." I figured that, at some point, they had to catch me.

We each had our own support crew for the Horny Toad, because there were very few aid stations. Lance Halsted, an old swimming buddy and part of my crew, rode next to me during the run. "They're 30 seconds behind . . . then 40 seconds . . . 45 . . . 1:05," he'd say. I couldn't believe it. I was pulling away from those guys! I mean, they were the best in the sport! It just blew me away, and I found myself racing more on adrenaline and excitement than training.

Needless to say, that was one of the most exciting victories I've ever had. I was starting to think I had a bit of talent for the sport. There I was, my third race ever, and I won $1,000. That was half a month's worth of lifeguarding right there. All my lifeguard buddies were pretty excited. They couldn't believe I had won.

I called my dad afterward and, all of a sudden, he showed a little bit of interest in what I was doing. Part of it was that I had won the race. But mostly, I think he saw that it was something I cared about. He could sense my excitement, he could hear it in my voice, he could feel it in the way I talked. And he realized he didn't need to ask what I was going to be doing in the future to earn a living. That didn't matter so much anymore.

After Horny Toad, I didn't race again in 1982 until October, when I did the Ironman in Hawaii. I didn't schedule anything else because I wanted to be

The Horny Toad Triathlon was in August 1982, and it was only my second triathlon. After the bike ride, I found myself with a 30-second lead over Scott Tinley and Scott Molina, the two best guys in the sport. I kept thinking they would catch me during the half-marathon run, but they never did.
Photo by Mike Plant

totally prepared when I got there. Come race day, I thought I was ready.

At the end of the Ironman swim, I found myself right behind Dave Scott, right on his feet. He got out of the transition area before me and picked up a minute or two pretty quickly. But I finally gained that back when we started hitting the head winds on the way to Hawi. I caught him just before the turnaround at about 55 miles. Out of deference to "The Legend," I decided to let him go through first. Maybe it was a

Do I look a little happy? You bet I was. All my
lifeguard buddies were gathered at the finish
line of the Horny Toad Triathlon, and in this
photo I'm about 10 yards from the first win of my
career.
Photo by Mike Plant

bit of a mistake, because right away he put another 30 seconds on me. He just sprinted through there and picked up that tail wind. I was working on gaining that back, but when I went to change into a big gear, my derailleur broke. I was concentrating so hard, I couldn't figure out what had gone wrong. Things were clinking and clanking. I looked back to find that my rear derailleur was loose, and all I had left was my 12, my hardest gear. I rode a little bit farther, a couple of miles more, but I realized, "Hey, this is ridiculous. I've got over half the bike to go plus the whole marathon. I'm not going to blow my knees out to just finish a race."

Mechanical failure. It's a stark reality. I had been euphoric, just being next to Dave Scott in the Ironman. But reality hit when my derailleur broke. I had to drop out. The whole reason I had trained all season was the Ironman, and now I wasn't going to be able to finish it. I sat on the side of the road and let it sink in. It was pretty heavy, watching my dreams race off down the highway, with no way to catch up with them.

I was tempted to just go out and run the marathon. I knew I could do it, but instead I hung out and tried to enjoy the day. Watching Dave Scott come down the finish chute was pretty emotional. I imagined what it would be like to be him. That would have been something!

2
ME AND MY DAD

*Some people are so sensitive to failure that
they try to avoid mistakes at all costs.*
—David K. Reynolds

I was born at home, on the living room table. We lived in a tiny shack of a house in Glendale, California, behind another house. At the time, my dad was doing lab work, medical research.

He went to medical school in St. Louis when I was five years old. Because he was in med school, we lived in a low-income housing project. There was urine in the elevator, and the walls were so thin you could hear the guy next door beating his wife and hear her screaming and crying. There was a playground downstairs, and I could look out and see it from where we lived. I was always afraid to go down there, though. When my mom bought groceries, she'd have to sit downstairs in the car and honk her horn until my dad went down to get her. It was unsafe for her to walk around by herself.

Those were my illustrious begin-nings. I guess all along I felt I was hope-lessly lost in a sea of the ordinary. I al-ways wanted to do something that would stand out, something others could look at and say, "That's incredi-ble."

When you're a kid, you have heroes, the kids who are most popular in school. I was never outstanding, not the brightest, the best looking, the biggest, the meanest, or the nicest. I looked at other people with a bit of jealousy. I was never the fastest either. Eric Bunje, my best friend all the way through high school and college, was always a faster swimmer than I. I could never beat him in the pool.

I always had faith, an idea in my mind that everyone has a special talent. If only he can find it, he will be unbeat-able, the best at something. For some, it might be a glorified talent—being the best runner, or the best tennis player.

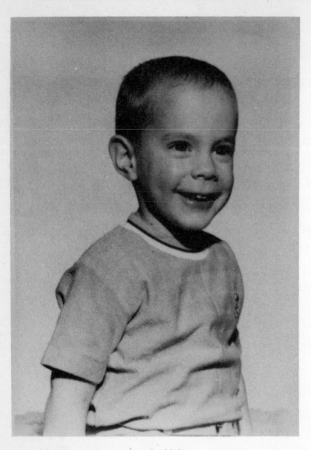

I know, I was one cute kid.

Other people sweep leaves off the lawn better than anybody else, or make the best pumpkin pies. I was your basic guy, but I was in search of my special talent.

My family moved from St. Louis to Sacramento and finally, by the time I was eight or nine, to Palo Alto, California.

I started swimming competitively in fifth grade and continued through junior high and high school. At the end of high school, I thought, "That's it." I wasn't really reaching the potential I thought I had. When I got to the University of California at San Diego, I continued to swim, but the coach I had during freshman year wasn't very

good. I swam maybe three days a week my first year at college, but I still qualified for the Nationals. The school wouldn't send me unless I qualified in more than one event. I said, "Forget that. I'm not gonna pay my own way to go to some race." So I quit swimming.

The following year, though, the school hired a new coach, and I decided to go out for the team again. I had been

Can you tell I'm a little excited? At 12 years old I've just qualified to race in class "A" events for the first time. And I did it three times in one swim meet!

swimming all my life, and the sport was hard to give up entirely. I ended up improving each of the remaining three years. I was never close to qualifying for the Division 1 National Championships or the Olympic Trials, but swimming is the kind of sport where no matter what level you're at, there's a niche that you fit into. My niche was NAIA Division 3.

Still, when you're in a sport, you want to feel like you could get in there with the big boys and compete. Even if you don't win, just making it to one of the top-level meets in the country or the world would be great.

Why did I swim? For a kid involved in sports, one of the big motivations is parental support. Your parents can get interested in what you're doing, and they appreciate your efforts.

I was a pretty normal child, needing approval just like all kids do. Initially, swimming got that for me. My dad was real excited in the beginning; he'd come to all the swim meets. But then he lost interest or got busy. His interest level and my ability to communicate what I was going through during all the different races and meets diminished at the same time. When I got to college, where I had my best successes in swimming (NAIA National Finals in 10 events), our relationship had reached a point where I couldn't communicate with him, where I couldn't tell him what it meant for me to be able to compete. Even when I tried to explain it to him, he didn't seem to understand.

So there I was. I had this device, this sport, to try to get a bit of approval, some attention, some love from the guy. And it didn't work. I'd talk about swimming, and then the subject would drift

Even though I did hit a grand slam during my one and only baseball season, I spent most of my time out in right field watching the clouds, and the balls, go by.

off a bit, and we'd end up talking about school, about what I was going to do after graduation. He didn't apply any obvious pressure, but I knew he would be excited if I became a doctor. Even though he swore up and down that if he had to do it over again, he wouldn't become a doctor, he still wanted me to follow in his footsteps.

Here I am with my mom after two important events. One is after an age-group swim meet, and the other is after winning the Nice triathlon.
Nice Triathlon photo courtesy of All Sport Photography

I started to feel like I had followed a well-known path, a safe trail, through grammar school, high school, and college. The idea was to get a degree and go to medical school. The closer I got to the end of the trail, the more I resented its narrowness, the classes you had to take, and the requirements. Some courses seemed useless at the time and even more so after I was done. I knew that college was a process of learning to learn, but I couldn't understand why the material couldn't be interesting at the same time.

During the summers, I was lifeguarding. During my senior year in high school, I left Palo Alto and went to San Diego to try out for a lifeguard job. A friend promised me that I'd like it.

"You get to work on the beach and get a tan, and it pays better than flipping burgers," she said. It was midwinter when we tried out, and I was in great swimming shape. There was really, really cold water (54 or 55 degrees) and big surf that day. I qualified, but thought, "Man, all these other guys are really good swimmers." I didn't do as well as I'd expected to. But I lifeguarded that summer and every summer through college.

When I finished college, I made my last stab at following the path I hoped would lead to approval from my par-

ents and satisfaction with my life. I took the Med CATs (medical school entrance exams). In the process of studying for them, I found myself resisting, I didn't want to study; it was a pain in the ass. Every time I had to go to the library to study tapes in order to do well on the tests, I thought, "What am I doing? Why am I doing this?"

I took the Med CATs and did well enough to get into medical school. I thought, "Here's another four years of med school plus three, four, or five years of internship and residency. Then I'll probably be caught up in my prac-

tice and still not be able to call my time my own." I realized I'd much rather be poor and have time to surf down in Mexico than make lots of money and have only a few weeks a year to do what I wanted with my time.

So, after college, I decided against medical school. I lifeguarded full-time for a couple of years starting in 1980. I went surfing in Hawaii and Mexico, and really enjoyed life. Lifeguarding was never something that I wanted to make a career of, but it sure was a good fraternity to be with.

Of course, my dad now understands

what the triathlon has come to mean to me. After I won the Horny Toad in 1982, he saw that I really enjoyed what I was doing. It made him look at his own life and recognize that there was a part of his job that he didn't like. He started to wonder whether it was worth it to make x amount of dollars if enjoyment and fulfillment were missing 90 percent of the time.

My dad eventually quit his practice and moved to Guam. He didn't earn half the money he did before, but he had free time to swim in the warm ocean, snorkel, and ride his bike. This was exciting for me, because I was finally doing what I wanted and doing it just for myself. And, without caring about it or wanting it, I started getting the love, attention, and appreciation from my dad that I'd worked so hard to get before. All those years of swimming, going to college, and taking the Med CATs were for nothing. When I finally started living my life for myself, I became a mirror for him. He was able to start integrating what I had learned into his own life.

3
TEAM J DAVID

We must be clear on what is controllable.
—David K. Reynolds

The infamous Malibu Triathlon came a month after my Ironman '82 fiasco. It was the first-ever triathlon offering big prize money. This was before I knew I was a prime candidate for the Hypothermia Hotel.

At Malibu, I had the worst time of my life during the 1.5-mile swim. The water was so cold, I thought I was going to drown and, for a lifeguard, that was really something. I made it to shore, but Scott Tinley, who was not a good swimmer at the time, passed me. Running up the beach, I was so cold, I couldn't tell what direction to go to find my bike. "Where are the bikes? Where are the bikes?" I yelled. They were right in front of me, and I couldn't see them. I was forced to drop out of the race.

Not long after Malibu, I was out training when my friend George Hoover came up to me and said, "How would you like to be on Team J David?"

"What would that mean?" I asked.

"We'll give you a salary, fly you around, and give you equipment."

I said, "Sign me up. Sounds a lot better than lifeguarding!"

My first Nice Triathlon in 1982, was also my first race under the Team J David banner. I had been a lifeguard, living hand to mouth, when the golden goose laid a four-egg omelette right in my lap. All of a sudden, I had a sponsor. They took care of all my travel expenses during that first trip to Europe. The time between dropping out of Ironman and landing in Nice was all of five weeks. In 35 days I went from full-time lifeguard to professional athlete.

Originally, the race was supposed to take place in Monte Carlo, but when Princess Grace died, a year-long moratorium was declared on festive events in Monaco. Consequently, that year the triathlon was switched from Monaco to Nice. Only a handful of American men and women were in France for the

My dad and I immediately after my 1987
Ironman finish.
Photo by C. J. Olivares, Jr.

brand-new event in a very young sport. The French people didn't really understand what a triathlon was. It was new in the States, but even newer in Europe.

I flew into Nice at night and couldn't see the countryside. After we arrived, Tinley and Molina wanted to go for a run. No matter what happens, those guys always want to go for a run. I thought I might as well go too. We ran along the Promenade des Anglais, which borders the Mediterranean. The Mediterranean was on one side and the bright lights of the city were on the other as we ran along a huge curving walkway. We'd just finished a 15-hour marathon flight that made countless stops, but we weren't tired. We were like wide-eyed kids, excited to be in

France, just soaking up the sights and sounds of this new country.

Before the race, we went on a few bike rides up into the mountains, and the scenery was incredible. We cycled on narrow roads that wind through the Maritime Alps. It was November, and the distant mountains had snow-covered peaks. We rode through ancient French towns where the houses were right on the street, up against the curb. The old French people had a distinctive, weathered look. Everywhere we went, we rode by historical buildings and castles. Huge areas were lined with hand-cut pieces of rock to protect against erosion.

George Hoover (right) has been one of my best friends over the years. He changed my life when he said, "Do you want to be on Team J David?" The next thing I knew, I was a full-time triathlete.
Photo by Mike Plant

On race day, the crowd of spectators wasn't what I would call stifling. But, remember, it was November in Europe, and it was 45 degrees out.

The water was also cold. I wore an insulated hood during the swim and booties, tights, and gloves during the ride. Partway through the bike ride, the course climbed up into the Alps. Before the climb, I could tell that I was going to get warm. I stopped, got off my bike, took off my tights, got back on, and headed off. I didn't think much about it at the time.

The course wound through hundreds of small villages. The descents were harrowing with some turns of more than 180 degrees. I'd come spinning out of the hairpin turns and blast into the little towns. The people lining the streets would hoot and holler, *"Allez, allez, allez!"* They didn't know who any of us were, but it didn't seem to matter. Competition is a universal language.

After the 65-mile ride, I caught Molina six miles into the run. While I ran with him, I noticed that he was real bouncy. I thought, "Boy, he's going up and down too much for a full marathon." I pulled up alongside him and said, "Hey, you're picking your feet up too high." He looked at me, but he didn't say anything. I thought, "OK, see you later." Then I took off.

After the race, Molina and I were sitting around rehashing the event. When I told him I'd stopped to take off my tights, he said, "You stopped in the middle of the race? You stopped and took off your tights?" He couldn't believe it. He couldn't believe I'd done a critique on his running style during the race, either.

"Remember when you pulled up next to me on the run and told me I was picking my feet up too high?" Molina asked. "I just looked at you and thought, 'Who the hell is this guy? He's been running for all of seven months, and he's telling *me* how to run?'" Molina ran track and cross-country all through high school and junior college. He was a real runner, and I was only a runner-come-lately. Maybe I should have kept my mouth shut for once.

Winning Nice set the stage for me in Europe. It was an exciting win. It immediately wiped out my disappointments in Hawaii and Malibu. The awards ceremony was much more formal than those for U.S. races. It was held in a huge, ancient, gilded room from the Renaissance. Everybody wore suits and ties. The mayor of Nice was there, and as a group of men and women from the United States gathered around him in the gardens, he commented that the race was fine for men but perhaps too hard for women. Needless to say, Lynn Brooks, the women's champion, and the rest of the contingent politely told him he might be more suited flying a kite than being a race critic. Nice showed me that I could do the long races and that if I just did my own thing, I was going to do pretty well.

The 1982 Nice Triathlon drew 450 athletes in a town where people had no idea what a triathlon was. Six years later, it's a huge event that draws athletes from all over the world. Four years ago, jogging was almost unknown in the south of France. In 1986, there was a freeway of runners along the Promenade. After holding this event for a few years, the local people must have decided that exercise for fun was a pretty good idea.

People from the small towns along the race route have become involved over the years. In 1986, each town's cycling club came out the morning of the race and cycled between its town and the next with the athletes in the race. They'd ride with you for a while and cheer and holler, and then ride home and accompany the next group of competitors. Families set up picnics along the route just to watch.

The Europeans have a different attitude toward road races. I'd call it a cycling mentality. They spend hours waiting for the Tour de France to come by, to see the cyclists for two minutes out of a whole day. The triathlon is a nice change for them because there is about an hour between the first and the last guy.

Team J David was very involved the first two years of Nice. It was a time when athletes were training full-time but corporate sponsors still hadn't been educated about the triathlon. Most still thought it was more of a freak show for crazy idiots than a vehicle to promote products.

J David sponsored Scott Molina, Scott Tinley, his brother Jeff, Bill and Julie Leach, Kathleen McCartney, and me. That was the core of athletes putting in a lot of time. J David helped us get through a period when no other sponsors were interested in triathletes. To grow, all sports need recognizable faces and personalities. J David gave us the opportunity to become recognized while the sport itself developed and gained national attention. If J David hadn't been there, I don't know what would have happened to the sport. J David's support gave all of us a chance to do the best we possibly could.

But Team J David was a double-edged sword. There weren't a lot of full-time triathletes at the time, but plenty of people wanted to be. There was resentment among those who were struggling to make ends meet. They felt we were getting an unfair advantage over everyone else. We were a stable of racehorses that were pampered and well cared for. Everyone else was out in the cold, cruel world facing reality. I have to admit, if I'd been on the outside looking in, Team J David would have looked pretty intimidating.

We had a lot of benefits. Our basic needs were taken care of, and that allowed us the training time to reach our potential. On the other hand, we had to put up with the negative press about J David. They called us Team Bitchin'. However, most of the people who complained about the team were also the ones sending in résumés and hoping a spot would open up.

A couple of years later, I found out that the J David Company received its money illegally. The firm went bankrupt, and it was called a Ponzi scheme. Jerry Dominelli may have helped us out, but it wasn't his money to help us out with. My first indication that something was wrong was when George Hoover came home and told me the company was going bankrupt. Dominelli was getting death threats over the phone. It made me realize that nothing is secure and solid in this life. You have to go with the flow and accept the changes.

During those J David years, I met many people. Some were rich and felt it put them in a position that was separate, better than everyone else. Unless you were equal to them in achievement, money, or star status, you were not a full human being. They were above you in their own minds. Others had already achieved some fame or fortune. I had looked up to them when I was younger. "Wow," I thought, "This person is famous. A star. He won a gold medal." When I finally met these people, they continually reminded me of all the great things they had done. Either they felt insecure, or they knew that at any moment, their achievements might lose their value. A third type of J David personality didn't care about the money or about being famous. These people had a strong sense of themselves and constantly gave to others and to the sport. They were extraordinary. I hope I learned from them.

4
MOTIVATION TIMES FOUR

All understanding begins with admiration of others.

—Goethe's Worldview, Ungar

One of the most important parts of my training is the motivation I get from guys like Scott Tinley, Scott Molina, Dave Scott, and Mike Pigg. If it weren't for them, I wouldn't have the incentive to push myself to the extent that I do. Having them always in my mind keeps me from getting lazy. There is always someone out there who can help push you. If you want to do the best you can, it helps to match yourself against other people. As much as there must be an internal drive to do the training and put in the miles, without their example, I definitely would not be where I am today.

Having a reliable set of training partners is invaluable. My day-to-day training partners, George Hoover and Julie Moss, help get me out the door and on the road. Whether I'm working out with them or just enjoying their company, they are my buddies, and

they keep me on the right track. I get bummed out occasionally, excited and nervous about events that happen or are coming up. Julie and George help me keep everything in perspective.

I train with Scott Molina in the summertime in Boulder, Colorado. It motivates me just to know he's putting in the long miles day in and day out year-round. I say to myself, "Scott Molina is out there, and come rain, snow, cold, or heat, he's putting in the miles." If I wimp out on a workout or get lazy, he creeps into my mind, and the thought of him makes me get out there and work. Molina really loves the physical effort. Someone asked him, "How do you get on your bike, day after day, and go for a 100-mile ride? Or go to the track and run intervals evenings after riding for six hours?" His answer: "When I get up in the morning, I just don't think about what I have to ac-

complish that day. If I did, it would become overwhelming."

I've learned a lot from that. I've learned to take each step as it comes. Molina has also taught me about patience, about taking the time I need to develop.

In Chicago in 1985, I finished second to my friend and training partner Scott Molina. Scott Tinley took third. And the other gentleman? Why, that's the late mayor of Chicago, Harold Washington. Downtown triathlons have become popular in many of the nation's major cities. The Bud Light USTS Chicago event drew 3,500 contestants in 1986.
Photo courtesy of Bud Light USTS

Molina has put in a lot of long years. If he's on a run or a ride and he's tired, he'll back off. He instinctively knows that if he goes too hard, he'll injure himself or be unable to do his workouts the rest of the week. Even with a big training group, when it can get a little competitive, he'll keep the ego in check and gauge his workout according to how he feels.

When Molina and I are flying to a race, he hardly ever talks about triathlons. He talks about other sports. He takes bits and pieces from other runners, cyclists, and swimmers and blends it all into triathlon. He talks a lot about his daughter. It's interesting to see someone who is so focused on a sport but receives a lot of his motivation for it from his daughter.

Molina also introduced me to the art of trail running. The first couple of years in the sport, I didn't run on trails at all. Every time I did, I had a hard time going down the hills because I'd twist my ankles. I thought, "Boy, trails and hills just aren't for me."

I did most of my running on pavement, along the San Diego coast. That's probably why I was injured a lot during my early career. Running on dirt is a lot easier on your legs than running on blacktop or concrete is, and all that pounding adds up. When a big race was coming up, Molina would say, "Come on, let's go for a run. I know a *great* trail, it's *nice* and *flat*. Come on, we'll go to Rancho Santa Fe or Black Mountain. They're *nice* and *flat*." The first couple of times, I actually believed the guy. Then I realized he was taking me out on these trail runs to thrash me before the big races. His joking around was all in fun but, because of his persistence, I became hooked on trail running. Now I do the majority of my running off road. I know it's saved my legs.

I've always admired Scott Tinley for his ambition to succeed in other areas as well as triathlons. He has always had some form of job other than triathlon. When he first started in the sport, he ran the Mission Bay Aquatic Center in San Diego. Then he worked for Second Sole shoe stores, organizing a triathlon team for them. When we were with J David, he helped organize and plan a lot of the activities. Now he owns a clothing line. Scott and his wife, Virginia, also devote a lot of time to their young daughter, Torrie Amber.

I'm kind of a procrastinator. There are days when after finishing an hour run and an hour and a half swim, I'll look at the clock and think, "Where'd the day go? I haven't done anything." Then I think of Tinley. I know he designed a new pair of shorts, had three business meetings, rode 80 miles, ran 10, and swam for an hour that day. Tinley trains year-round and keeps his body fit all the time. I need a bit of a break in the winter. I couldn't do what Tinley does. By mid-January, he's already done a few of his long rides, and I know he's been doing long runs every weekend. I'll think, "The season's getting closer. I'd better get on it."

Some mornings, I just don't want to get up. I've had my 10½ to 11 hours of sleep. I mean, how much more can you get? Then I think about Tinley already being done with a 12-miler, and that gets me out of bed real quick.

Tinley's strong personality has gotten him far in this sport. He's also improved the state of triathlons in general. During the early years of the sport, if something wasn't done quite right, he'd let people know. Everyone else sits back and tells the race director this was nice, that was nice. Tinley will

During the 1980s, the Big Four of the triathlon world have been (from left to right) Dave Scott, Scott Molina, myself, and Scott Tinley. Between the four of us, we have won eight Ironman titles, five Nice triathlons, the World's Toughest Triathlon twice, and four Bud Light USTS National titles.

Photo by C. J. Olivares, Jr.

say, "Hey, it was nice, but there were things in this race that I didn't like, that were dangerous. They have to be cleaned up for next year." I respect him a lot for putting himself on the line like that.

His single-mindedness has helped, too. On an 80-mile ride, a lot of people tend to stop and eat something after 40 or 50 miles. They start gabbing and eating slowly. Then, the next thing they know, they've been off the bike 30 minutes. Tinley will keep you honest. After two or three minutes, he's on his bike pedaling around the parking lot ready to go. He'll give you a minute, and then he's off. He's going to get it done.

I don't know Dave Scott quite as well. It's hard to know him as an individual. People know what he's done in the races, what he's accomplished. But

when I think of Dave, I think of his ability to focus. He can have a terrible start to a season and lackluster performances all year long. But when it comes to an important race like the Ironman, he puts it all together. He can say, "OK, this is it. This is what I'm go-

The boys, Scott Tinley (center) and Scott Molina (right), battle it out with Glen Cook of England at the Desert Princess Biathlon in February 1987. I found out early in my career that I just can't race as often or train as much as Molina and Tinley have over the years. I learned that to stay healthy, I needed to develop my own training program.
Photo by C. J. Olivares, Jr.

ing to do, and this is what I am focusing on." The rest of the time, he's doing clinics and talks, and I know that cuts into his training time. He must say, "It's a trade-off, but this is what's got to be done."

When it comes down to the final race, you'd better watch out. Each year, people think Dave is over the hill because he raced poorly in the shorter events. They figure he's out of it for the longer races, too. Each year, I tell myself this guy is not washed up. He's shown me that you have to take time out and do the things that further your life and your career. Then focus when it's time.

Dave has a major battle of philosophy with the other triathletes. He says, "I'm up in Davis, California, training on my own. It makes me a lot tougher because I'm simulating race conditions every day when I work out." People aren't around to keep tabs on how he's doing in his workouts. When he shows up at the races, all of us wonder how Dave's going to do, what type of shape he's in. Is he going to be hot or cold?

Most people feel that training partners motivate you when you're tired or burned out. They can get you over the humps. Obviously, though, Dave's training philosophy works very, very well for him. Personally, I'd go nuts if I had to train as much as he does in an environment without people to draw on for motivation. His philosophy focuses on one important element: when it gets tough in a race, you have to draw on yourself.

And then there's Mike Pigg. I got to know Pigg quite well the summer of 1987. There was a week off between the Bermuda Triathlon and the USTS Denver race. So Pigg came and trained with us in Boulder. He showed up at

high altitude to train with a group of people who were already used to it. He hammered day after day after day. He's always working out. I thought, "My God, is this just youthful enthusiasm?" Suddenly I realized this guy is good at what he's doing because he's so determined. He's trying every technique he can in his training, his diet, and his racing to figure out what is best for Mike Pigg. That determination makes him tough.

To be honest, I was glad when the guy left Boulder at the end of the week. I was starting to get worn down trying to keep up with his workouts. But Pigg is one of the nicest guys around. He's thankful for everything that comes his way. Because of triathlon, he's gotten to travel and do things that he never dreamed of when he was growing up in Arcata, California. If he doesn't win, he's motivated to train harder.

Pigg's development in the sport has been in stages. In 1986 he was satisfied with a certain level, and then in 1987 he needed to perform at a higher level to be satisfied. Next year, he'll shoot for an even higher level. He has a plan for becoming the best in the business, a mapped-out plan of attack. I'm a little more haphazard in my training; I go more by how I feel. In a lot of ways, that's really good, because you can avoid the pitfalls of injuries. But sometimes I'd like more of that systematic attack on my training that Pigg has. He's only been in the sport a few years, and I'm learning from him.

I outraced Pigg most of the time this year, but that doesn't mean I didn't draw any knowledge from him. It's like the teacher teaching the student who's teaching the teacher. That brings me to our climb up Mount Evans.

Mount Evans in Colorado is one of

the hardest cycling climbs you could imagine. At over 14,000 feet, it's the highest paved road in North America. The road is really steep and rutted at the top, and no matter when you climb it, it's *always* cold and windy. It's one of the supreme efforts. When you've done it, you feel like you've survived the ultimate test of human endurance.

Mike Pigg was going to ride Mount Evans. He was going for it, doing what he could do, testing his body to see what it could take. So Molina, Pigg, Ken Souza, and I set out for the climb with him. With that climb, he taught me not to be afraid to try anything. He rode it to see what would happen out there. And he surprised himself with how great he felt the whole way.

It's this kind of strength I can draw from when I come up against something that makes me apprehensive. To be successful is just a matter of following the 3 M's. And what are the 3 M's, you ask? Motivation . . . motivation . . . and motivation.

5
BE YOUR OWN HERO

The arrow that hits the bull's-eye is the result of the one hundred previous misses.
                                    —David K. Reynolds

Kids are like a Colorado morning, clean and pure, brand new. When you were very young, everything was exciting. Of course, some things upset you, and you felt weak and vulnerable at times. But when it came to learning, you had so few expectations that everything was wonderful.

I remember how excited I was when I was first learning how to read. The other kids had a week or two head start on me in the reading book, and I didn't even know the alphabet, because we had recently moved and I started school late, after classes had already begun. It was a little frustrating, but still exciting. Once I started to get the hang of it, it was even better. "Wow, I can do this—I can read! 'Look at Spot. He's running fast to his friend Dick!'"

So I learned, and whatever I did was great because it was more than I had been able to do before. Once I learned the basics, the material became more complicated. I pushed to get good grades and score high in the national tests. I had to go to college, but you can't get there unless you get good SAT scores. Then there were expectations to deal with and that's when the anxieties start to hit.

When there are expectations, you're locked into the climb to the top. Maybe what you've learned and what you want to learn are exciting, but you can get a bit confused as the motivations start to change. Soon you're developing skills that will help provide you with a job and an income, channeling your energies toward either college or employment. Unless you're fortunate to have clear goals, you'll probably face some dead ends, performing tasks you don't really want to do.

If you keep going, you may find yourself resisting what you're doing. But

57

people tend to keep on, looking toward "success" as if that were a goal all by itself. If you keep going, and the anxiety and pressure continue to build up, you'll start to think, "What if I fail? I'm not doing well enough, I used to be better. I'm not going to get where I want to go." You may get through this inevitable period of self-doubt and resistance only to move on to the next step. You get married and buy a house, then a new car. All of a sudden, there's a baby to put even more pressure and responsibility on you. . . .

My racing started as something I wanted to do purely for myself. I was like a kid experiencing the joy of learning to read. Every little bit of progress was great, everything I learned was super. There was no sponsorship. No one had any expectations of what Mark Allen was going to do.

Then a little recognition crept in. There was an article in 1982 about a dark-horse contender in the Ironman, Mark Allen. The recognition built on itself, and I started to establish standards for what I wanted out of myself. I pushed my expectations increasingly higher. I thought about my performance, my racing, my training, and my public posture. I thought that by doing just what I wanted, I could skip out on the responsibility end of the life cycle and avoid the whole pressure game.

It didn't work. Here I am, in 1988, triathlon season number seven for Mark Allen, and I've put myself under more and more pressure. I received a lot of exposure over the past year with a Kellogg's Pro Grain cereal television commercial that featured me. Kellogg's set me up with TV news interviews, talk shows, and radio interviews before any races I did, so I could plug Pro Grain

Before the 1983 Ironman, I was lean and mean.
Photo by Mike Plant

and spread the word about this great cereal out there.

One jam-packed week in 1987, I went to New Orleans to do a coach's conference on a Tuesday, and from there to Baltimore for a race that weekend. After running Wednesday, I gave a clinic at Lynn Brook's Fleet Feet running store. Thursday I did a little working out and tons and tons of radio and TV promotions. This went on and on until race day. I hardly had any time to train the whole week before the race, and I was burned to a crisp from all the appearances. I was feeling scattered because I didn't have the quiet time I need to compose myself and get myself together before race day.

When you're a kid, you handle pressure differently. You do as much as you want to do, and then you sit down and pout, cry, or have a temper tantrum. When you're older, you develop self-discipline and end up doing more and more of the things you don't want to do. Even if you're doing what you want to do, you can get overloaded. You keep trying to convince yourself that what you're doing is what you *need* to do, that it's the best thing for you.

So there I was. Not what I'd call my ideal training week, not the best way to prepare for a race. But I'm trying to build an athletic event into a career. And, along with performing well, I have to be able to speak in front of a camera, relate to a group, and maybe even write an article. I'm going to have to do more than just race to show people what I'm all about. People can relate to the event to a certain extent, but you have to go beyond that.

Look at Ivan Lendl. He's a classic example. One of the best tennis players ever, but because he doesn't throw temper tantrums, because he's quiet and reserved, he doesn't have the following someone like John McEnroe develops. McEnroe is often offensive, but he's more popular because he has that public side. I want to be visible enough so that people can recognize me and can relate to what I stand for.

All my life, I've been building myself inside, striving. Even when I change from one avenue to the next, I'm always building on my past experiences. Those enable me to move on to the next venture, even if it's completely different. The basic skills and concepts I have about myself come from life experi-ences. That helps me avoid repeating mistakes and move faster with more efficiency and balance.

When in your life can you stop trying to build on something else and just say, "It's time to put it in neutral," and start living in the moment? When you're 65, do you just retire, hang out on the porch, and play golf because there's nothing else to do? Or do you retire because you finally realize, "This is my life, and if I can't sleep in, if I can't relax and take a nap when I'm tired, what's the point?"

There's nothing wrong with having the drive to build and move forward, to move onward and upward. You need a goal to get from point A to point B. But how old am I going to be before I can stop psyching myself up to do and do and do? When do I get back to the childlike fullness of looking at something I've done and getting satisfaction from it without it having to be something that will move me toward the future or get me to another spot?

There are a million stories about guys 20 years old, just about out of college. "By the time I'm 40," they say, "I'm going to retire. I'll have my house, my car, my Lear jet, my kid, and I'll fly anywhere I want to go." Some of these guys even attain all that. Then they look back at the 20 years between 20 and 40 and think, "I have all the things I wanted at 20, everything I thought I'd enjoy ... and they mean nothing. I want that feeling I had when I was six years old, lying in bed, and my stomach did backflips because it had snowed that night. What happened to that kind of excitement and enjoyment? Why do I have to spend a thousand dollars to fly somewhere else to be happy? What am I missing?"

I don't want to end up like that. I don't want to wait till I'm 40, or 65, before I give in to life and allow its own beauty to be my satisfaction. A while back, I suddenly realized that that's what I was getting involved in. It's so easy to do, especially when you have to make ends meet so you can keep eating.

So, now I'm approaching what I'm doing from a different perspective. I don't do what I do just for the sake of building up and moving on. Instead, there must be an intrinsic beauty and enjoyment in the action, no matter what it is. I'm still working on this new attitude, but for me, that should be pretty easy. I spend the majority of my time training in the mountains, on the trails, or in a swimming pool. I can always find relaxation and beauty through the motion of my body, the movement of my muscles, and the excitement each cell feels when the blood rushes through it.

What I've been trying to do is to visualize my chores, my duties, my goals and aspirations. There are things I want to do. I need to do them with enjoyment now so that if I give up anything in the process, there's been more than enough satisfaction in exchange. It's the attitude that makes the difference.

A lot of people ask me how I can go out there day after day and do the training necessary for a triathlon. They see a five-, six-, seven-hour day of hard physical activity as impossible or at least unpleasant and avoidable. It's baffling to them.

I find that, yes, there is something inherently boring in training. Essentially, the ultimate goal for each day is to surprise yourself by doing something you didn't think you could do, and doing it without resistance. If you can achieve your goals each day with as little resistance as possible, you're going to be totally satisfied. For example, in the pool, when you're doing a 500-yard swim, you can think, "Oh, I've got 350 to go. Oh, man, I've got 175 to go." There's resistance in that approach. Or you can think, "I've gone 350 yards . . . I've gone 400 yards." In the second way of thinking, in each moment, you're thinking about what you are doing. You aren't thinking 250 yards ahead. You are where you are.

When starting something new, it's best to take the attitude of a kid. You see something you want to do, then you find out how to do it. If you want to learn how to ski, you rent skis and take a lesson. The attitude of a child makes anything that happens full of excitement. If you go slow, that's exciting. If you go too fast, that's exciting. If you fall down, that's also exciting because you've learned what not to do. The body puts it together without any conflicting ideas from the mind.

The same approach works for endurance sports like running, cycling, or swimming. You go to the bike store and get a bike. Someone helps you adjust the cleats and the seat. A friend who's been doing it for a few years takes you out on a ride. Maybe you haven't ridden a bike for years, but it feels great. The wind is in your face, you're breathing hard, feeling the sweat. It's a new sensation for the body, and it's exciting. This is what it means to start out as a child.

Or you may be the type of person who starts out with expectations, with what I consider more of an adult attitude. You say, "OK, I've seen Jean-

Claude Killy ski on film, and I want to ski like him." You're embarrassed that you don't already know how to ski, but you get the equipment. You don't want a friend to take you out because you're afraid he'll see you fall. You go out and, first time down the hill, you get some extra speed up and fall down. You're angry, shocked, and marginally frustrated, because you didn't ski like old Jean-Claude the first time down the hill. Depending on your level of perseverance or commitment, you either give it up or, if you're bull-headed, overcome all the frustrations that stand in the way and learn the sport.

You can take either the attitude of a child or that of an adult going into anything new. Children are quick learners. That's because they have the ability to do something without judging it. They look at what works, look at what doesn't work, and reject the latter. They move on quickly, without mulling and stewing over an experience that somebody might consider a failure. The attitude of a child will take you wherever you want, to any level of achievement you desire. The adult attitude slows progress, even though eventually you can reach high levels. It's a cycle of success and failure, and you pay a high price in frustration and stress.

But even the guy who starts out with the childlike attitude doesn't always keep it. Once someone tells him, "You've got talent, you should do something with it," he starts having expectations. He wants to build on his achievement instead of enjoying the moment. He starts to work on skills and regiment his training—and soon he's experiencing the same things the guy with the adult orientation has all along. All of a sudden, he's vulnerable to failure.

You don't have to settle for saying, "Whatever I did today is just fine." But you can experience your own level of accomplishment in whatever you've done. Trying to get out of yourself the best you can do at that particular moment, and letting that be the satisfaction is much better than being like the guy who wins a race and is upset because his time wasn't great. For example, in the 1984 Olympics, Rick Carey won the gold medal in the backstroke, but was upset because he didn't set a world record. If he knew he put out 100% that should have been enough of an achievement in itself.

With success, the pressure builds, creating higher and higher expectations until even winning isn't worth the cost. It may not be until retirement age that you realize that a great performance is fine but no more important than the other areas in your life. Whatever level you achieve on a given day is fine, and you just go for it to see if you can surprise yourself. It's amazing how much you can accomplish when you aren't carrying around that five-pound bag of expectations. Getting to whatever level you can is important. But soon you'll get caught up in the path leading up to the goal and suddenly realize you're enjoying the quest itself.

It's impossible to win everything, and you can't win forever. Someone younger and stronger will eventually come up on your heels. So you have to become your own hero. Instead of saying to someone else, "Hey, if only I could do what you can do," give yourself credit for what you can do yourself.

It's important to eliminate the negatives. Instead of thinking, "Today was a lousy day. I didn't make my planned 100 miles. I skipped 20 miles on the

No this wasn't an ad for *TQ (Triathlon Quarterly)*. The scene was the President's Triathlon in Dallas, my first spring race of 1987.
Photo by C. J. Olivares, Jr.

bike and didn't do the run," try thinking, "I was really tired when I started out, but I made it through 80 miles on the bike, and I held a good pace all the way. That was a great day!"

When you have a really good experience—when you run faster than you thought you could or close four business deals in one day—try not telling anyone about it. When you do that, you become your own hero. It's enough to make you explode, because you've filled yourself up with yourself. And when you've done that, no one can take that away. When you don't tell anyone, you've got incredible energy inside that's all yours.

It's the same when you have a really bad day. Don't tell anyone that your day was a total piece of garbage, that you didn't finish your workout, that you blew the deal, that you wimped out. Don't let anyone know about it. No one can read your mind and realize that you had an awful day. Then watch what happens inside yourself. Slowly but surely, instead of trying to get sympathy from somebody else for that poor day, you're going to start having fewer and fewer of them. Pretty soon, they'll be great days. The body doesn't want to keep that all to itself, it wants good things to share . . . and you'll have them.

6
THE CLASSIC RACES, OR "OGDEN, UTAH? NO BIG DEAL."

The surest way of finding the limits of our abilities is to act.

—David K. Reynolds

Some races are milestones. Others just beat the crap out of me. But they're all personal classics.

My first classic race was the Horny Toad Triathlon in August 1982. It was my first win, and I couldn't believe it. I won $1,000 and beat the two best guys in the sport. Plus it was half the distance of the Ironman.

After the race, I found out that I was going to be on the cover of the *San Diego Running News*. I couldn't wait until it came out. I walked into a running store in a big shopping center, and the issue was sitting in the doorway with my picture on it, big as life. I wondered if the girl behind the counter was going to recognize me. So I sat there for a while and picked up a copy of the issue. I was looking at it and looking at her. "Does she recognize me? Does she see that I'm the guy on the cover of this thing?" She didn't even notice. It sort of put things into perspective. I thought, "OK, you won a race, you got on the cover. Now go back to the drawing board. You're not exactly Kareem Abdul-Jabbar yet."

USTS TAMPA

The USTS Tampa at St. Petersburg (1,500-yard swim, 25-mile bike, 6.2-mile run) in April 1984 was also a classic race, not because the matchup was so close, but because for the first time I dominated a race.

The USTS circuit was picking up steam on the East Coast. St. Petersburg was the first race of the season, the first year of a big season opener, and everyone was serious and gunning for it.

The day before the race, Tinley and I took a spin around the bike course. We did about 30–35 miles, which is a lot of mileage for the day before a race. I got behind Tinley; I was spinning, hardly putting any pressure on my pedals. I was almost in a hypnotic state—no matter how hard he went, it felt exactly the same to me. I was relaxed, strong, and confident.

The day of the race, I woke up and thought to myself, "I'm just gonna play with these guys. I'm going to make 'em chase me." I came out of the water with the lead group and hammered the first few miles on the ride. After the race, Molina told the press, "I just couldn't hold on to the guy when he took off." I came off the bike with a big lead and by the time I got to the turnaround on the run, I was 1:15 ahead. I knew there was no way they could make that up because I felt too good. That was my second breakthrough: racing unintimidated. It was a big thing for me.

You need to be really clear when you're racing. If you're nervous about all the other guys, forget it. You won't have the best race you can. You can only race scared so often. When you're racing scared, you're stiff, nervous, and not clear in your thoughts. When you're intimidated, the competition's got you beat. They've taken the power from you mentally and physically. When you have your own energy and that's what's driving you, you can use the others as catalysts to bring out the best in you. Then you're going to race to your potential.

OGDEN, UTAH, HOME OF BARRY MAKEROWITZ

I had never heard of Barry Makerowitz until I traveled to Ogden, Utah, for what turned out to be another personal classic race in June 1984. It was the first race where the race director flew me in and put me up. I did a prerace clinic, where I talked about training and racing and got paid a little money. I was excited about doing that. It was a new position for me to be in. I'd done well the year before, winning the Nice Triathlon, and I was having a good year so far. So the race director had asked me, "Hey, want to come out here to Utah and do our little race? It's a 1,000-meter swim in cold water in a lake outside of Salt Lake City, a 35- to 40-mile bike with a fair amount of downhill, and a 13-mile run." I said, "Sure, no big deal. Go to Ogden, Utah? That sounds great. How good could the competition be in Ogden, Utah?"

When I got there, someone said, "Oh, yeah, you should keep your eye on Barry Makerowitz, number 123." I thought, "Yeah, OK, no big deal." I was feeling pretty cocky, pretty sure of myself with what I saw as a small-town event. I trained normally that week, no taper, no time off. Ogden, Utah? No problem, right?

But the race was at altitude, which I hadn't taken into account. Breathing starts to get a little tough at over 5,000 feet. I came out of the swim OK and had a really good bike ride. I was almost six minutes ahead of the next guy, whoever that was. I was so confident, I was racing in my training shoes. Ogden, Utah? Ha! It was an out-and-back run course that went up and down and up and down. It was *really* hilly. There was no flat in it anywhere. I was running a comfortable pace, expecting to put even more time on these people. When I made the turnaround at the 10K point, I thought, "Just for insurance, I'll start my watch and see how far back the next guy is." And right away I see this guy—he's charging like an elephant. He's moving, hammering, locomotion in motion. I look at his number, and it's 123—Barry Makerowitz.

I couldn't believe it. He was six minutes behind me at the start of the run, and here he is one and a half minutes back with six miles to go. He made up four and a half minutes in the first six miles! All of a sudden, I realized that my little cherrypick race was turning into one of the toughest things I'd ever done. I had to pour it on just to stay alive. I went harder than I've ever really had to go, right until the finish.

There were people along the side of the road, and I'd ask, "How far back is he? How far back is he?" They'd look at their watches and answer me with blank stares. I was getting a little bit annoyed. I figured everyone wants to help out the leader of the race, right? Wrong. Makerowitz got to within 10 seconds of me with one final hill, then a 200-yard downhill to the finish. I knew if I could just make it to the top of the hill first, he couldn't beat me. I barely made it to the top ahead of him. I won, but it was the closest race I had all year. You should never underestimate the local talent. It turned out that the people who weren't giving me splits were his cousin, his aunt, and his sister. It was an all-out Barry Makerowitz fan club!

GULF COAST TRIATHLON, PANAMA CITY

I had been winning my races, such as the USTS Miami, by a pretty good margin, and I was ready for the first-ever Gulf Coast Triathlon in Panama City in May 1983. Dave Scott was there, and it was the first time we had met since Hawaii, where my derailleur broke in the middle of the Ironman. "OK, this is it," I

thought. "I've got a good shot at beating this guy."

I came out of the swim with him. Dave, Molina, and I were all together. The bike course consisted of two 30-mile loops. It was the first time any of us had raced on a looped course, and it was the first time the three of us were together at the beginning of the bike. It turned into a cat-and-mouse game, with no one willing to be the aggressor and take the lead. In every race up to that point, I'd thought only to go as hard as I could on the bike then do the same on the run. This race was different. There was a sense of head-to-head competition.

I felt OK during the first lap, but halfway through the second lap, Molina started to pull away. I thought, "He's going way, way too fast. No way he could go that speed and still run 13 miles at the end." I decided to let him go. Dave didn't seem too concerned or too aggressive, either. I started to pull away from Dave, and I thought, "Hey, this is it, man. I'm gonna beat this guy for the first time. I'm gonna do it and do it good." I came off 1:15 ahead of him and that far behind Molina. I was a little nervous though. Dave is a good runner when it comes to longer races. I caught Molina in the first two miles. Dave was still 1:15 behind.

Then all of a sudden we heard reports that he was picking up 20 seconds a mile on us. I looked at my watch, and we were running 5:30–5:40 per mile. Here it was 95 degrees, in the early afternoon, during the heat of the day in Panama City, Florida, and Dave is running a 5:15–5:20 pace. I thought, "I can't believe that guy is running that fast." When I found out how fast he was running, it made me nervous. I knew that he had beaten me and I didn't have the experience or self-confidence to know what to do about it. At about mile 8, he finally caught me. Dave has a way of coming by you with a bit of finality. He doesn't look at you, and he doesn't acknowledge you. I tried to keep up with him for a while, but he can maintain that intensity just beyond the point that breaks you.

It was partly my own inexperience that caused me to lose that race. Dave Scott beat me although he hardly put any time on me during the last couple of miles. Here was my chance to beat The Man, and I couldn't do it. It was some consolation to stay ahead of Tinley and Molina, but it was Scott I wanted.

The third time I raced Panama City in 1985, I had the same experience with Ken Glah. I came off the bike, and some guys were ahead of me. I was right with Ken but behind Dale Basescu. Right away, Kenny tried to break me. He put one and a half minutes on me in two miles. I thought, "It's over, he's won the race." Then I thought back to how Dave had done it two years before. "No," I reevaluated, "the race isn't over. In this sport, nothing's written in stone until you've crossed the finish line." I told myself to relax, to keep my pace, to push the limits and see what happened. After putting a minute and a half on me, Glah kept the same lead for the next five miles. Then I started gaining it back, a little bit here, a little there. I hit the turnaround with a couple of miles to go and he was dying. My patience was starting to pay off. At mile 11½, I caught him, and there was no way he could hang on to me. I went by him with no regrets, no nothing. No "Sorry, Kenny. Here I come." I learned that trick from Dave Scott.

Perhaps if Dave hadn't beaten me the way he did in 1983, Ken would have won the 1985 race. I was fortunate enough to have the confidence to keep going.

USTS CHICAGO

Sprint races were significantly faster in 1986 than they had been the year before. I had never done the Chicago race, and Molina was the defending champion. I remember feeling a little bit intimidated by him. This was during his full-on strength days when Molina never seemed to lose a USTS race. "OK," I thought, "for me to win, I'll have to put out a major effort." When you know the level you have to rise to, you do it. You just do it. I came out of the water ahead of Molina by 30 seconds, got on the bike and hammered. I'd lost the Nike Triterium to Molina on the bike the week before, and I was not going to lose that way two weeks in a row.

Up to the turnaround on the bike, I was in the lead. I was putting out 180 percent, going as hard as I could ever go. I thought I was pulling away from everyone. I couldn't imagine anyone riding as fast as I was. The way the course is laid out in Chicago, after each turnaround, you're able to see all the competitors coming back your way. Mike Pigg was maybe 15 seconds behind me, with Tinley and Molina 5 seconds behind him. I thought, "I don't want to just sit out here like a carrot for those guys." I slowed up a bit, and Pigg caught me. "OK," I thought, "the race is back on." I stayed with Mike the best I could, trading the lead with him a few times. I guess I was getting a little too close. I didn't think there was anything

The Bud Light USTS Chicago offers a fast course and topflight competition.
Photo courtesy of Bud Light USTS

wrong with our positioning, though. A draft marshall was following us on a motorcycle, but he didn't say anything. I assumed that from a drafting standpoint, nothing was going on.

Pigg came in 20 seconds ahead of us on the bike. Tinley, Molina, and I all rolled into the transition area together. It's formidable, running with those two guys.

Right away, Tinley was off the back. Molina and I had been training together at altitude, and I think it was

paying off. Molina and I then caught Pigg, and we were on our own.

A few years before, at the Crystal Lite Triathlon in New York, the race had come down to a sprint finish between Molina and me. I thought, "Oh, boy, here we go again!" We ran step-for-step the entire way. It was cat-and-mouse in the sense that each was waiting for the other to make the first move. But it wasn't cat and mouse in the sense that we were going maximum speed the whole way. When you're going as hard as you can go, it's difficult to think about going faster, about surging from that speed. But to drop a guy, that's what you have to do.

There was a gradual upgrade to the finish. That's where I surged. Molina stayed right on my shoulder. I thought, "How am I going to shake this guy?"

I kept the surge going as we took a sharp right turn. Now there were only 200–300 yards to the finish. I was the first to round the last straightaway, and the minute I hit it, I poured it on with everything I had. I was going so fast I was starting to get the high-speed shakes. I was almost out of control.

The final surge was just enough to break Molina. As I was coming toward the finish line, I thought, "This is too intense. I could not race like this every weekend. I just couldn't do it. It hurts too much." As I crossed the finish line, everyone cheered, and I thought, "Right on . . . I won the race." Then I heard, "And here comes Mark Allen, who has been disqualified for drafting on the bike." I thought, "What are they talking about?"

Then the disappointment set in. The marshall came up. He said, "Look, you were disqualified for drafting on the bike. You were too close to Pigg." It

During the bike ride at the 1984 Ironman, I didn'
eat or drink nearly enough. I just tuned out the
rest of the world and concentrated on spinning
my chain ring. Before I knew it, the bike ride was
over and I had a 12-minute lead on Dave Scott.
Photo by Mike Plant

I ran strong for the first few miles down Alii Drive,
but things were different when I hit the lava
fields.
Photo by Mike Plant

At about mile 13, Dave Scott went by me like a freight train. It's a long walk back to Kona when you start to hurt so early in the Ironman run. I ended up finishing in fifth place.
Photo by Tracy Frankel

went on into a whole long argument. I appealed, but I lost.

It was the race effort of my life, and I was disqualified. It took a while to put the disqualification behind me and say, "OK, just use that race as your strength, and don't get all upset and bummed out about it. You've got to use it in your training and racing for motivation."

A few months later, I saw some pictures in *Triathlete* magazine. In most of them, I would say I was not drafting. In others I was close, closer than I had thought. Sometimes racing distorts your perception of what is close and what the distances really are. In this one, I think they made a bad call. Maybe I was a little bit too close to Pigg, but in my opinion, it wasn't drafting because of the way the winds

I started out the day not feeling very good. But somehow, as the 1985 Nice Triathlon heated up, so did I. Having people near you riding motorcycles and carrying cameras can get you pumped up, too. On a long ride like Nice (75 miles), it's important to be as self-contained as possible. Notice I have two water bottles on the bike plus food in my back pocket.
Photo courtesy of All Sport Photography

were blowing. By the rules, though, it was drafting.

I can now understand players' disappointments with a football call or a baseball umpire's decision. You've got to live with it. If the man says you screwed up, you screwed up. You've got no choice but to move on. I felt like the guy who was convicted of treason just because his words were misinterpreted. But the bottom line was that I had a great race. And once again I knew that I could beat Scott Molina.

YOU NEVER KNOW

My body has felt great before certain races and my energy has been at an all-time high. Then during the race, something would happen, and I'd end up falling apart. The Ironman in 1984 was like that. During the bike, I felt like a

machine that would never run out of fuel, totally efficient and incredibly fast. By the time I reached the bike-to-run transition, I had a 12-minute lead on Dave Scott. That lead held as I ran through town on my way out to the lava beds. I turned right to run up the quarter-mile hill out of town, and my tank immediately went from full to empty. It was as if the sight of the lava fields spread out before me was enough to rob me of every ounce of gas I had in my body. In a matter of minutes, I went

I was amazed that after starting out feeling so bad, by the end of the ride I still had a chance to win. Scott Tinley and I came off the bike together and then ran down Rob Barel of Holland. Finally, we caught the leader, Scott Molina. It came down to Tinley, my old training partner, and me. I was eventually able to put some distance on Scott for my fourth straight Nice World Triathlon Championship.
Photo courtesy of All Sport Photography

I sure felt a lot better after Nice '85 than I did
two years before. First I cooled myself off. . . .
Photo courtesy of All Sport Photography

from racing to surviving. With 15 miles
to go, it can seem like forever between
aid stations when you walk and jog
those last miles.

Those are the worst kind of races,
the ones where everything that can go
wrong does. But every once in a while,
the day will surprise you. You'll feel like
quitting before you even get wet, and
the day ends up being one of your all-
time best.

. . . and then I waved to the crowd.
Photo courtesy of All Sport Photography

At Nice in 1985, I woke up race morning feeling like I had the flu and barely able to get my body out of bed. If it had not been race day, I would have turned over and gone back to sleep. I struggled through the two-mile swim and the first set of climbs on the bike ride. All the top competitors were somewhere up ahead. Then, suddenly, my competitiveness started to assert itself. I kept telling myself that I felt strong and fast, even though the reality was quite the opposite. I guess I was pretty convincing, because slowly my body began to respond.

By the end of the bike, I'd caught Scott Tinley. He and I set off in pursuit of Rob Barel from Holland, a minute ahead, wishfully chasing Scott Molina, seven and a half minutes further up the road. By the run turnaround, Molina had only three minutes on us, and Barel was weakening. With six miles to go, Tinley and I dropped Barel and were poised to pass Molina. With five miles left, Tinley and I were on our own. A day where I started out feeling sick was ending with a chance for me to win my fourth Nice World Triathlon Championship. I dropped Tinley, won the race, and learned never to predict the day's outcome by the way I feel in the morning. Nice 1985 reinforced that old Yogi Berra axiom one more time: It ain't over 'til it's over.

NICE 1983

My win at the 1983 Nice Triathlon was another classic event. I'd like to be able to tell all about it, but there's one problem. I don't really remember much of what happened that day. The basic facts are these: I went into the last few miles of the 20-mile run with a 10-minute lead. By the time I made it to the finish, I was only 2½ minutes ahead of Dave Scott. Unfortunately, the day is a total blur in my memory bank because I was suffering from severe dehydration. But plenty of photographers were there to record my plight for posterity. As far as I'm concerned, the following photos are what I call my 'Wide World of Sports" montage. Rather than the thrill of victory or the agony of defeat, they show an up-close and personal look at the agony of victory.

In 1983, I returned to Nice, France, as the defending champion. During the early portion of the bike ride, Scott Molina and I were right together. Note the difference in our climbing style. I like to stay seated, and Scott has a tendency to get out of the saddle.
Photo by Mike Plant

Sometimes it's hard to focus on just racing where the people are cheering and the countryside is so incredibly beautiful.
Photo by Mike Plant

I still look strong, and I'm finally able to get my hands on a bottle of water. Dave Scott and Scott Tinley were both having the same problem getting fluids. We were all dehydrating badly.
Photo by Mike Plant

The run during the 1983 Nice Triathlon was one of the hardest things I've ever done. I reached a point with about three miles left where my eyes had problems focusing and my body totally shut down. In the first photo, I still had a big lead and looked fine. I was just cruising along the French Riviera with my entourage of motorcycles, mopeds, and bicycles. But there was very little water on the course, and my body was starting to feel the effects.
Photo by Mike Plant

I was literally out on my feet, like a punch-drunk
fighter, as I walked and jogged those last two
miles to the finish. It seemed like an eternity.
Photo by Mike Plant

At the finish, Frank Shorter (right), the gold medalist in the 1972 marathon, and an unidentified race official, helped to keep me upright. Shorter was there with NBC Sportsworld.
Photo courtesy of All Sport Photography

I guess it's safe to say I was a little out of it at the end. Here I am in the medical tent after the race. Not quite the picture you'd expect of the conquering hero.
Photo courtesy of All Sport Photography

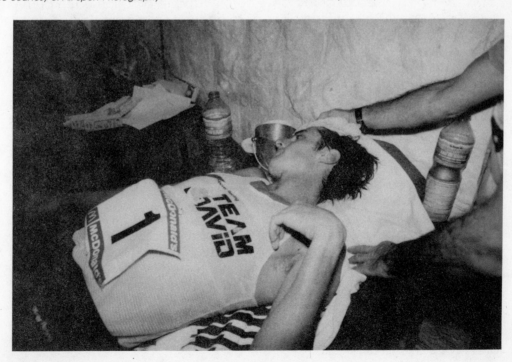

FUN AND FROLIC IN CYPRUS

Just after the 1984 Olympics, the International Management Group (IMG) invited me to an International Superstars competition in Cyprus. I was really excited to be in that part of the world. I could feel the history, the mythology, and the gods. Everywhere I went, there were Greek artifacts, pieces of old roads, and columns from ancient ruins. The Superstars competition was similar to the one you've seen on television, except the competitors in Cyprus were athletes like West Germany's Rolf Dannenberg, a gold medalist in the discus; New Zealand's Ian Ferguson, a gold medalist in rowing; and England's Robin Brue, a swimmer who set a record in the 200 individual medley. The events in Cyprus were different from the American Superstars events. There were polo, cyclecross, the 100-meter dash, clay-pigeon shooting, weight lifting, rowing, an obstacle course, and an 800-meter run. The run was held on an ancient oval track that hadn't been used since the time of the Greeks, centuries before.

So here I was, Mark Allen, world-class triathlete, in against all these other world-class athletes. We were able to try all the sports and choose one to eliminate. The guy who was going to win was the one with the best eye-hand coordination and the fastest fast-twitch muscles. Since I do long-distance events, I don't major in fast-twitch. Nor do I have the strength for weight lifting or any God-given reservoir of eye-hand coordination. I was the kid who used to live in right field.

I arrived in Cyprus four or five days beforehand to practice each of the events. The organizers wanted all of us to train on the horses. They didn't want all 10 athletes falling off our horses in front of the TV audience and the spectators in the stands. We spent a fair amount of time each day learning how to ride a horse, hold a polo mallet, and hit the balls. By the end of the week, I wasn't the best guy out there—but I wasn't anywhere near the worst.

My best event was the 800-meter run. For a lot of those guys, that was a long way to go. I finished second to Robin Brue in the 800 and second in the cyclecross, too. I thought I'd be able to win it, but a two-minute event was a little different from what I was used to. In rowing I finished in the middle of the pack, but I called it a victory because I didn't tip over. A lot of guys couldn't make that statement.

But the classic was polo. It was the cornerstone event of the competition because the organizing was done by the British military and held on the military's polo fields. The British have a strong interest in Cyprus and, as we all know, a pretty strong interest in polo. They decked us out in complete polo outfits with the boots, the pants that come partway down your legs, the riding hat, and the little whip. If they had taken a still photo, no one would have been able to tell us from the Olympic polo players. But stick us on horses, put a camera in our faces, and it was a little different.

The horse I rode on the day of the competition was the same one I'd been practicing on all week, and he could tell something was up. When I got on him to warm up, he was sweating and nervous.

The bleachers were full of spectators that day. A couple of people went before me, and then it was my turn. "Here is Mark Allen . . . triathlon champion," they announced. "Come on horsey . . . come on horsey," I said, easing him onto the field. Then the horse took off and sprinted full blast out onto the field. I was yanking on the reins and shouting, "Whoa! Whoa! Hold on, buddy, hold on!" There was nothing I could do. He wouldn't stop. All of a sudden, he put on the brakes, and I went flying over the front of the horse. I was totally out of the saddle, hanging for dear life onto this poor horse's neck, looking right into his eyes. He was sweating, and I was sweating. I could hear the British in the crowd say, "Ohh, my God. These Yanks don't know how to ride a horse. Get him off the field before he embarrasses all of us."

I humbly remounted Mr. Horse and ended up hitting two balls wide of the goal. That was the last I wanted to see of the Superstars. But I had one more shot.

The last event was the 100-meter sprint, and, well, let's just say I wasn't leading the parade at this point. I felt the least I could do before I left town was beat old Rolf Dannenberg. He smoked cigarettes and was a massive hulk. One of the nicest guys you could ever meet, but a hulk just the same. I thought, "I may not be a sprinter, but I can beat this guy. He'll be lucky if he even gets out of the blocks."

Somehow we were paired off together. The gun went off, I looked over, and old Rolf was already five yards ahead of me. By halfway, he was 10 seconds ahead in a 100-meter dash! By the end, I was catching him, but it wasn't enough to run down old Rolf. Hats off to you, fella. You got me in the 400-meter dash. If it had been 110 meters, I think I might have winded him.

I ended up fifth out of eight athletes. The Superstars competition made me realize an important fact of life: Being good at one sport, or even three sports like some of us are, doesn't make you good at every sport. Staying humble is the name of the game.

7
STAYING IN BALANCE

God gave us the nuts. But he will not crack them for us.

—*Goethe's Worldview*, Ungar

Have you ever wondered why someone like the Scott Molina of old could go hundreds and hundreds of miles on the bike each week and run hard day after day and not get hurt? He trained every day and raced once or twice every weekend for five or six months straight, year after year, and he won practically every race he was in. How can someone's body take all that pounding?

The key is having balance in your life.

Part way through my first year competing, I thought I had a good shot at being one of the best in the sport. To do that, I felt I had to imitate what Molina, Tinley, and Dave Scott did in their training. I forgot to take into account the fact that I started running only two months before my first race and had run only 100 miles in my entire life. I didn't have the base to do the mileage

they were doing. I shouldn't have expected to copy their training schedules and stay injury-free. But I was oblivious to the concept of building a base, and I kept getting injured. Not only didn't I have the physical base, but I didn't realize that I needed to modify my lifestyle in order to handle the additional physical stress on my body. All of a sudden, I was trying to fit my training schedule into a 40- or 50-hour-a-week job as a lifeguard.

At the time I started training, I was going out with Bunny Stein. I would come home from work and go for a run. When I got back, I was tired. But there was this other person in my life who had wants and needs that I wasn't meeting. Energy that I'd previously put into supporting and consoling Bunny and enjoying her company was now being diverted into training, racing, and recovering.

I needed to modify my lifestyle in order to keep everything in balance so I wouldn't get injured, so I could perform well, and so the rest of my life wouldn't fall apart. This might sound obvious, but I don't think people give it enough credence.

When you train, your body gets tired. When your body gets tired, it needs time to rest and recover. If you don't give it time to recover, any of three things will happen: (1) You'll lose interest in the sport because it's just too tough and you're tired all the time. There's no fun or enjoyment in it if you're always dragging yourself around town. (2) You'll get injured. (3) You'll get sick. A stress on the body is a stress, no matter if it's physical or mental. I think we all have a certain tolerance level, but beyond that, everything starts to go haywire. That is what happened to me.

I had consistent training days for a time, then I started to get a little rundown. But I had a vision of how many miles I had to go to get where I wanted to be. I would be maybe two days away from the end of a particularly hard workout period, and my body would be telling me, "Back off, you can't go two more hard days. Stop today." But I wouldn't listen. I'd wake up in the morning feeling tight, stiff, and out of energy. I'd reset the alarm three times because the first two would seem too early. The third time, I figured I had to get up. Something in me was saying, "God, I really wish I had a day off. I wish I could just take it easy and not have to run and swim." I'd do it anyway. The next day, I'd start to get out of bed, and my knee would hurt so bad I could barely move. I'd be achy and sore, and I would feel like I had the flu.

All of a sudden, I had what I asked for—time off—but definitely not in the way I wanted. I didn't want to be sick or injured. You've got to watch what you ask for, because you're going to get it.

A lot of people ask how you can tell whether you're being lazy or are really tired. I ask them, "When you wake up in the morning, how do you know if you've had enough sleep?" You have to learn what the body is telling you and learn to be realistic. There are days when you're tired and worn out. What I do is get myself up and at least get out the door. If I'm just feeling lazy that day, once I'm out the door and going, I'll feel fine. I'll feel able to do it at that point. But, if I'm fatigued, I'll get out the door, and 10 minutes later I'll feel the same. Twenty minutes later I'll feel worse, and an hour down the road I'll feel awful. That's a good sign that today's a day to turn around and take it easy, take a nap, walk the dog, fix the car, or go to a movie.

Now, you can talk yourself into just about anything. You have to get yourself into some semblance of a routine so that you do experience consistency in your training and allow yourself to get stronger from that consistency. In doing so, be alert to signs of being overtrained and overtired. If your pulse rate is five or ten heartbeats above normal in the morning or you have a decreased appetite even though you've been increasing the workouts, it might be time to lay off. Feeling hot when you are resting and ready to go to bed, having a hard time going to sleep at night, and restless sleep are all signs of overtraining.

When you start a training routine, no matter what the level, your goal is to get stronger. To get stronger, you need to

Part of the excitement of professional sports is getting to meet some of the more famous characters of the world. The one between Kirsten Hanssen and me in Chicago is that world-famous party animal, Spuds McKenzie.
Photo courtesy of Bud Light USTS

stress yourself. After you rest from the stress, your strength will increase. You don't get stronger from going hard; you get stronger from the rest you get *after* you've gone hard.

Ultimately, during your rest period, you want to feed your body everything it needs. This means not only the right food, but also the right thoughts and the other right things that you need to care for yourself. This will help you minimize the time it takes to recover. When you do that, you can handle an increased work load and have more energy left over for the rest of your life.

Remember, sports is not absolutely everything. It's just one piece that fits into balancing out the whole puzzle of your life. I think the quote goes, "Continually remind yourself of the equality of all things." It's good to keep that in mind, so you don't let yourself get too out of touch when you're training and racing.

The Chinese have a theory on balance in life based on the idea of yin and yang. These are the two forces that make up our being, yin representing female energy, and yang the male. Any activity we do requires an output of these energies, some requiring more of one than the other. For example, a physically demanding motion, like lifting a weight, may require a lot of yang energy, whether done by a man or a woman. A finer movement, such as the stroke of an artist's brush, may require the use of yin energy. This is very simplified and by no means absolute. The same motion done by two different people could possibly draw on the male energy in one person and the female in the other.

One day recently I was thinking how this might apply to triathlons and keeping them in balance with the other aspects of my life. Triathlons are to me a very yang activity, definitely male. When you're out there racing, with sweat dripping down your face, going as fast as you can for 8, 10, or 15 hours, that's masculine, yang energy. The same goes for the training. There's not much yin energy in that. For me, yin activities are going to the movies, reading, relaxing, resting, taking a Jacuzzi, getting a massage, or doing things that involve color and texture.

How do Tinley and Molina seem to train and race endlessly? How do they balance out that endless output of yang energy? Tinley helps to design clothes for Scott Tinley Performance Wear. Working with cloth, colors, and shapes helps him balance out his physical output. Molina? He's always reading books and magazines. To me, that's balancing the opposite side of the physical.

I reach points where I get sick of training. I'm tired. I'm not going to recover and feel better by doing activities that require a similar form of energy. For example, it wouldn't be relaxing for me to go out and ride my mountain bike. Even when I surf or ski, I don't do it aggressively, especially during the season. It's more a form of relaxation. You have to balance out that artistic or intellectual side. One of the best things for me is to go to a movie, to just sit there and relax. It's calming, entertain-

ing, and nurturing. No output of energy is required. Reading is also a yin kind of energy.

And what's the absolute best thing for me? Let's say I go for a two-hour run. I come home and have a nice breakfast, shower, then curl up in bed. I'll pull the blankets up over my body. Then I'll go into that state where the body starts warming up. I'll lie there in bed, almost asleep and feel that position, the most comfortable position in the world. I'll hold off going to sleep because it feels so good. I'm warm, and I've done my workout, and then I go to sleep. I don't need to sleep long, maybe 20 minutes or half an hour. I'll wake up feeling totally refreshed. After intense workouts, when you go to sleep at night, think nurturing thoughts, anything positive and relaxing. Make a conscious effort to relax, feeling warmth and energy. Fill the body with that before you go to sleep. Allow yourself to relax into it. The more you're able to relax into it, the more quickly you go to sleep and the more deeply you sleep.

Balance even affects the food I eat. When I'm not working out hard, I can eat a lot of things, foods that are maybe harder for me to digest. As the body gets fatigued, you need to eat foods that are easier to handle. In the off-season, I can eat lots of chicken, fish, or quesadillas. I can also eat lots of brown rice; no problem. I chow it down and feel great. But when I'm feeling tired, I need a grain that will give me just as much energy as brown rice but is easier for me to digest. Then I go to millet or quinoa.

I like foods that fill me up with that male energy—spicier foods. To me, a cucumber is absolutely the weakest food that God has put on the earth. I mean, why eat it? It doesn't do a thing for me. I'll probably offend the Cucumber Council, but that's the way it goes. Give me a raw grated beet over a cucumber any day.

Getting back to balance, rest, and recovery, pay attention to your needs to balance that yin and yang energy. You'll find that you'll have a quicker recovery if, instead of hammering yourself all day every day, you go home in the evening and read a bit from your favorite magazine. It helps you to recover. This may sound crazy, but you really recover faster. You can do harder and longer workouts.

A few weeks before I race, I've got to have workouts that are totally physically demanding to satisfy my yang side. I thrash and push my body. I go to the point where I think, "What am I doing this for? This hurts way too much." Workouts like that give me that male energy I need for racing.

I've never been able to put my finger on the ingredients of balance. Hard days and easy days, that's your balance. Yin and yang. Feminine and masculine. The first year I wasn't injured was 1987. I didn't have an injury that kept me out of training for more than a day or a day and a half, and I didn't get sick before any races. Two years ago, I was sick before every single race. There was an imbalance somewhere. For me, a major part of avoiding sickness is pinpointing what I need to do. I've been able to increase my work load and go harder when I need to.

I ran 10 miles the day before the 1987 Vancouver Triathlon. Until then, I would never, ever have thought of running 10 miles the day before a race. That year, it felt like the thing to do. I felt I did it at a speed and in a way that put energy into my body rather than taking it away.

It can be difficult for women in sports to balance the yin and yang energies in their lives. Former Ironman winner Kathleen McCartney put on makeup before going out to train. Whenever I saw her race or train, she had some sort of makeup on. The artistic act of putting on makeup was probably her way to keep in balance. She was doing something requiring yin energy. There she was, busting her buns, sweating a ton, and breathing like a horse. But she had balanced that feminine side of herself. It's OK for a woman to be a jock. But when there comes that moment of conflict within, then there's a problem. If she maintains that balance, male and female energy ceases to be a problem.

After winning Kauai in October 1986, Scott Molina went home and broke bones in his foot during a training run. He said, "This is the best feeling that I've had in a long time. I don't have to train." He'd obviously gone a little bit overboard and was out of balance. To get that balance back, he had to take time off and rest.

Part of balance is allowing yourself to recover. Sometimes late at night, I'll think, "I'll never be recovered by the morning!" Then I'll think, "Why shouldn't I be? Why shouldn't eight or nine hours of sleep be enough?" I'll tell myself, "This *is* going to be enough sleep." Sometimes I'll be rolling around in bed, thinking, "I'm not going to be rested. It's already 3:00 A.M., and I have to get up at 7:30 A.M." Right when I'm feeling that restlessness, I'll make my body go limp in the bed, almost like someone has knocked me out. I'll lie

One of the greatest rewards of staying in balance is a great big win. I've just won the **Bud Light USTS** in Chicago.
Photo courtesy of Bud Light USTS

there limp in the bed and tell myself I'm absorbing sleep, that I can absorb more sleep in four hours than I ever thought possible.

One time I was on the plane and I was really tired. I thought, "Wouldn't it be great if time could stop for everybody else, but that I could continue on in a timeless space and get as much rest as I needed? Then when I woke up, I'd be all rested." I closed my eyes, and all of a sudden I saw a square waterfall suspended in space. It wasn't water, but time that was falling, coming down and tumbling straight into space. A mist was coming off the corner of the waterfall. It was a reddish pink color, and in that mist, suspended right there, was timelessness. So, I put myself where time was suspended and took a nap. When I woke up 20 minutes later, I felt great, like I'd had a couple of hours of sleep. I guess sometimes time does stand still.

Depending on what your goals are, you should be realistic when talking about recovery. You've got to work out hard, period. To do well, you have to be consistent, put in the workouts and put in the time. There is no short cut from novice to expert. But you can decrease that time by reducing any resistance you have to your training. Pay attention to what your body wants and needs. No doctor can tell you how much you need to rest, and no coach can tell you how hard or easy you need to work out.

When it comes to my recovery program, I think of the yin and yang. I'm no guru who sits in his room and meditates. But I do relax and try to keep myself on an even keel. I listen to my body to find out what I need to do to stay that way.

You can only do so much training. After the season is over, after the Ironman, I've had so much physical training that all I want to do is something mental for a month or two—like reading or going to the movies. By the middle of the winter, I feel like training again. And by spring, I'm ready to race.

8
THE STREAK

How may one get to know oneself? Never by contemplation, only, indeed, by action.
—Goethe's Worldview, Ungar

For me, going into each triathlon season after the winter break is like starting over. Because I'm a professional, a lot of expectations go along with my performances. My time at the top is not forever, but when will it end? Will it be this year? Will I be faster than last year, but slower than the rest of the guys? Will great personal performances be overshadowed by even more outstanding racing from the other men? Will my sponsors keep supporting my efforts if I fall short of last season's results?

The 1987 season was no exception to that inevitable period of self-doubt. The winter before, my workouts went as planned. My excitement for the sport and my love of it were still there. But by the late spring, I hadn't raced in several months, and I needed to get out and put it all to the test.

Mike Pigg had been the early-season scourge of the triathlon circuit, virtually blowing away everyone on the bike, then holding onto his lead with some greatly improved running. Filming a TV commercial for Kellogg's in March had set my training back a few weeks. The season looked long enough without going into the first set of races under-prepared, so I didn't surface on the triathlon circuit until Dallas, at the President's Triathlon on May 30. A newcomer, Canadian-born Andrew McNaughton, almost stole the show with a fantastic bike split, but I was able to catch him with less than a mile to go in the run. Richard Wells from New Zealand, who had destroyed the world in Perth, Australia, at the World Sprint Championships in January, was in the field, but he was never a factor in that race.

Next came Avignon, France, followed by the USTS Atlanta on June 20.

Above: Atlanta was the first time Mike Pigg and I met in 1987. It was the beginning of a great rivalry. Mike is an outstanding athlete, and we had some outrageous races together.
Photo courtesy of Bud Light USTS

was looking to redeem himself for some early-season losses. Wells had a great swim but couldn't get moving on the bike. I passed him early on. Much to my dismay, Pigg was having a great bike ride, and he passed me early, only

Below: What would you do if you saw this guy coming at you? Well, I hope you said you'd go harder. Because that's exactly what I had to do. Mike Pigg and I raced against each other in Atlanta, Baltimore, Chicago, Vancouver, Bermuda, and Hilton Head, South Carolina. I was able to hold him off until the Bud Light USTS National Championship in Hilton Head. But what's wrong with five out of six?
Photo courtesy of Bud Light USTS

Atlanta was supposed to be an "easy" race for me, a cherry pick. But Pigg, Molina, and a few others decided at the last minute to show up. It was my first chance to see up close what Pigg could do. He caught me halfway through the 25-mile bike ride, but he couldn't get much more than a 20- or 30-second gap on me the rest of the way. I had a great run and won the first of our many confrontations in 1987.

One week after Atlanta, on June 28, was the USTS Baltimore. Wells was there, along with Pigg and Molina, who

Before the season, I thought Atlanta would be an easy race. I should have learned a long time ago that there is no such animal. *Every* triathlon is hard.
Photo courtesy of Bud Light USTS

10 miles into the ride. This time he pulled away with ease. I had to make up one and a half minutes on the 6.2-mile run if I was going to win. Mile after mile went by, and no Pigg in sight. Finally, halfway through, I could see him up ahead. By mile 4, he was within 15 seconds. At 4½ I pulled up behind him. He surged, and I thought, "Oh, no! He was just resting until I caught him." I held his pace, and he backed off. Then I tried a surge and, 25 yards later, the race was mine.

At Baltimore in 1987, Mike Pigg had a 1-minute, 30-second lead on me after the bike. I thought there was no way I could catch him, that my winning streak was history. I was wrong. I caught Pigg with about one and a half miles to go.
Photo courtesy of Bud Light USTS

PIGG AND ALLEN, THE BEST ROAD SHOW IN TOWN

Atlanta, Baltimore, Chicago, Vancouver. What we have here is a classic in the making. Well, yes, I am talking about the Vancouver race itself, which provided one of the most beautiful settings ever for a world-class triathlon. But I'm also talking about a classic rivalry, one that could, if it keeps on like this, end up right there with some of the best sports one-on-one matches of all time. Jack Nicklaus and Arnold Palmer . . . Jake Lamotta and Sugar Ray Robinson . . . Joe Frazier and Muhammad Ali . . . Eamonn Coghlan and Steve Scott . . . Bobby Knight and Everyone. And now we have Mark Allen and Mike Pigg.

Mike Pigg is the new kid on the block. During the early season, he took everything in sight. He won in Tampa, Miami, Memphis, Houston, and Bakersfield. You name the city, he won the race. Mark Allen, on the other hand, was busy lining up a major endorsement deal with Kellogg's Pro Grain cereal. When he wasn't shooting commercials, he was somewhere else posing for posters, signing autographs, or speaking to the High School Coaches of America. When the five-time winner of the Nice Triathlon flew to Atlanta in May, he was looking for a tune-up race, not a major confrontation. But what he found instead was this red-hot kid named Mike Pigg breathing fire at the starting line, just waiting to knock off another one of those Big Four–type characters. He'd already beaten Scott Molina often enough to own the guy, and Dave Scott and Scott Tinley were finding it impossible to stay in the same county with the kid on the bike. Pigg Power reigned supreme, and the young man from Arcata, California, with his groupies (the piglets) in tow, was the new king of triathlon.

Mark Allen's nice, low-key tune-up race in Atlanta was turning into something much different, something Allen wasn't particularly looking forward to. But, after Pigg gained his customary lead during the cycling leg, Mark Allen did something Pigg hadn't seen up close and personal for quite some time: Allen ran him down. The two then flew off to Baltimore to do it again. This time Pigg had a big lead off the bike, and when he ran a sub-34-minute 10K at the end, you would have sworn that the race was in the bag, that it was bacon-and-eggs time again. Wrongo. Mark Allen ran a 32:08 10K after getting off the bike, and although he didn't put Pigg away until five miles, he did what he had to do to win. At the USTS Chicago, the scenario was the same. Pigg with a lead off the bike, Allen with a lead at the tape.

So when the two of them flew to Vancouver for the Vancouver International Triathlon on August 9, even though Scott Molina, Dave Scott, Scott Tinley, and many other top men were in the field, those in the know were in town looking for a little P and A—a little Pigg and Allen, the best road show in town.

There is a natural line of progression in the Mark Allen–Mike Pigg rivalry. First Mark Allen beats Pigg out of the water. Then Pigg passes Allen on the bike and tries to put as much space between them as humanly possible while bent over his Scott handlebars like a human pretzel. Finally, Mark Allen catches Pigg somewhere in the run. But in Vancouver, a funny thing happened on the way to the swim-to-bike transition area. The lead swimmers were directed off course, and before he knew it, Mark Allen was suddenly behind Pigg coming out of the water. "$%*(@#$@! Is that Pigg?!" he yelled to Scott Molina after catching him early into the bike leg. Molina nodded that yes, indeed, that figure up ahead cycling toward the horizon was the elusive Mike Pigg. Mark Allen could tell that it was going to be a long day.

"He's usually 40 seconds behind after the swim," Allen said later. "I knew right then that I had to catch him on the bike, or otherwise I could just forget it." Allen caught Pigg, and the two of them took turns surging away on the rolling hills that make up the 25-mile Vancouver bike course. With Molina already a minute back by the turnaround, it was definitely a two-man race. And with the run 12K rather than 10K, the magic arrow in the sky had to be pointing toward Mark Allen.

"Running felt good right off," continued Allen, "I figured I would run hard for the first two miles. When I looked back at mile 2, Pigg was right there." So what did he do? He ran hard to the 4-mile mark, figuring Pigg had to be off his back by then. "I looked back at mile 4," he said, "and he was still right there!"

Allen had good reason to be surprised. While Pigg is usually a good runner, he was great in Vancouver. He had the run of his life. But with the temperature 15 degrees cooler than either of them are used to racing in, Mark Allen wasn't just out for a casual jog himself. "I went through six miles in 30 minutes flat," remembers Allen, "and I felt very good."

Five-minute pace for a 12K run after a 25-mile bike ride? The sport of triathlon has obviously moved into a new dimension. It's a place where only the fittest—and the fastest—can survive. Only two men have scaled that peak to reach the summit. The Big Four have now been whittled down to two. Their names are Mike Pigg and Mark Allen. At the moment, they are in a zone all their own.

—Bob Babbitt

Swimmers emerge from Lake Michigan in the first leg of the Bud Light USTS Chicago race.
Photo courtesy of Bud Light USTS

Things were starting to look good. My training was paying off, and I was fortunate to feel strong on race days. The USTS Chicago and the Vancouver Triathlon added two more wins to the list, but Bermuda, on August 16, was the next weekend. It had the biggest purse of the summer for a sprint race, $100,000, and everyone would be ready, including the Americans, the Europeans, and athletes from Australia and New Zealand.

The weather around Bermuda was less than cooperative. A hurricane had passed within miles of the island the morning I was to fly there. Flights had been delayed, overbooked, and canceled. My flight took off from New York several hours late in an attempt to make it to the island. The flight was flawless until we started our descent. Just before the actual landing, we hit some incredible turbulence, the pilot hit the engines, and I was on my way back to New York. The next day, I finally made it to Bermuda. But my bike and luggage were somewhere in the Baggage Twilight Zone.

I figured one day of rest would be OK. No bike? No big deal. It would make me sharp for the race. By mid-afternoon the day before the race, I was starting to get nervous. Still no bags, and still no bike. I begged and borrowed the essentials from other athletes and the local bike shop. It was midnight, the morning of the race when the airlines called and said that my bags had arrived. With about four hours of sleep, I woke up, got my luggage, and put my Schwinn together. At that point, I didn't think I could have a great race, but at least I had my equipment.

By race time, I'd convinced myself that a lousy race was out of the question and that I could live on any amount of sleep—or even no sleep—for one night. I wasn't too concerned with the outcome. I decided that a great performance would mean never giving up during the race. It's easy to back off when all the normal preparation hasn't gone your way.

Every moment of the race was better than I could have expected. A good swim, strong bike, and a smooth run gave me another victory. Pigg was second again.

After Bermuda, Mike Pigg was thinking about training in Boulder, Colorado. He used a break in his racing schedule to come check it out. He loved it and decided to move out for the remaining two months of the summer. This was prime training time for the Ironman, and we used it to the fullest. Several hard weeks took their toll on us. Finally, Hilton Head was looming just one week away, and I felt the need to back off. I knew Mike wanted to win that race, and lots of other guys would focus just on Hilton Head. Race day came, and Pigg had one of his best races of the year. He outbiked everyone in sight, then ran his fastest 10K of the season. In the process, he ended my winning streak.

I felt some disappointment when the streak came to an end, but it helped remind me of my own limitations. It's easy to feel strong while winning. The test comes when I'm not. Losing reminds me to keep triathlons and my life in perspective; it lets me know I'm a person above all, not just a triathlete.

9
MARK ALLEN'S SAUSAGE PRINCIPLE

*We are born fighters; we will find something
to oppose. If we cannot find a worthy foe, we
create one, even if that foe is ourselves.*
— David K. Reynolds

Sometimes you have an idea of how you want a race to go, what you want to get out of it, and how you want to place. In my case, I want to win the whole thing. Ironman is always a thousand times more than you could ever imagine. When you feel good about your performance, then the feeling is great. When you do poorly, that too can really be magnified in yourself.

There were six weeks between the race in Bermuda (August 16) and the National Championships at Hilton Head (September 27). I spent that time training specifically for Ironman (October 10). I needed that period to focus, to put in the longer miles and not worry so much about my speed and being fresh every weekend for the shorter races.

My philosophy during the hard training is that, when I'm out there, I'm just going to tough it out. If I get tired,

that's fine, I'll back off tomorrow, but this is the time to learn how to dig deep, because that's what I'll have to do in Hawaii. I have to learn to go beyond the point where I start getting tired.

At the Ironman, after about 50 miles on the bike, your body starts to get tired. When you get to the run, you're worn out and hot. The thought of going another 18, 20, or 22 miles has no appeal at that point of the race. Those pre-Ironman workouts, when I go way beyond comfort, help me deal with the lava fields and not back off. I need to stay focused, to keep the pace up, keep the momentum up, and keep the energy in me. I have to be aware of what I'm doing at all times, and be alert enough to know when I'm going too fast or too slow. Then I'll have the best race I can out there.

Mike Pigg moved to Boulder right after Bermuda and was the guy who

Triathlons tend to start early in the morning. There's nothing like standing on the beach in a skimpy swimsuit waiting for the sun to rise. Personally, I like events that start a little later in the day.
Photo by C. J. Olivares, Jr.

helped me along. Before Ironman, I need to do that long mileage, and since Pigg was also gearing up for Ironman, we trained together daily. Twenty-one-year-old Kenny Souza was also part of our training group. He was always hanging in there, always ready to train—he's a machine, an incredible rider and runner. He would start every workout with us, but he might not finish it. If he was feeling good, though, it was your day of pain, not his, because he would just push the pace until you dropped.

During our Ironman training, we decided to go east from Boulder, because it's flat, like Hawaii. Souza, Pigg, and I would ride out past the cornfields on the old back roads. We could go 10, 20, 30 minutes without seeing a car. God save you if you ever got a flat tire out there. You could be stranded a long time. Those rides were getting us mentally acclimated to Ironman conditions, save the heat. We would go all out, 40, 50, 60 miles, then turn around and do it again.

It's enjoyable, testing yourself day after day, week after week, asking, "Am I getting faster, am I getting stronger?" The key is to push yourself beyond the comfort zone but still be able to absorb the training. Anyone can go out and thrash himself to death until he can't move, but that won't make him stronger.

We all need to get stronger. That's what world-class marathoner Rob de Castella, who also trains in Boulder, does in his training. He gets his body used to this kind of "hypermileage" by doing an over-distance run about five weeks before his marathon. That gives him time to recover, and his body gets used to being out there longer than during the actual race.

Five weeks before Ironman, I ended the week by doing a long run with Julie Moss. She did four loops and I did five around a 5½-mile reservoir outside of Boulder. My run was 27 miles, and each time around I went a little bit faster. My pace was faster than I would go in Hawaii. I ran for as long as I thought the Ironman marathon would take me, and I felt incredibly good the whole way. My body felt stronger than it had ever, ever been. Up until that year, if I went 22 miles on a training run, I would have been really thrashed and felt like I was on the borderline of injury. This time, with 27 miles, only the last 20 minutes were difficult.

Mike Pigg heard about it, and the very next day, after he won the USTS San Jose, he did the same run. Mike Pigg running 27 miles? I realized at that point that I was going to have my hands full in Hawaii. Not only did I have Dave Scott to deal with, but Mike Pigg would be there, too. And I heard through the grapevine about the incredible mileage Tinley was putting in before Ironman. He felt it was *his* year to win it. And who knew about Dave Scott? I didn't see Dave for weeks at a time. When he didn't surface at Hilton

Head, I knew he was going for the Ironman. The Ironman has been his career, his whole life. And he was going to be ready.

During this training period, I was getting progressively more fatigued, even though I was able to train hard day in and day out. The closer you get to the end of the long training, the harder you go. "Keep going," you say to yourself, "I've only got three long rides left, only two, only one long run."

About a week and a half before Hilton Head, Souza, Pigg, and I did our final long training ride at a place called Golden Gate Canyon, which is a series of three climbs. Pigg and I dropped Souza on the way out, on a long flat stretch. He obviously wasn't warmed up, because he just couldn't get going. We waited a while, but when he didn't show up, we started up the climb. Mike and I were both kind of tired, a little bit beat. It was a Saturday, and we thought we'd take a leisurely cruise up the canyon, which was about 20 miles of climbing.

We were two miles into it, when Souza came up behind us and left us in the dust. I had my heart monitor on, and I knew we wanted to stay aerobic—steady and slow—because we'd been doing a lot of anaerobic workouts on the longer rides just to get used to a real fast pace. I thought, "Nah, I'm not going to chase him. But maybe I can stay close and still stay aerobic." I didn't chase him but was able to keep him even at my pace of 155 beats per minute. All of a sudden, Pigg decided to bridge the gap.

We caught Kenny, and we hammered and we hammered and we hammered. Up we went, around and around. "OK," I said to myself, "I know the top is coming up, I know it's coming up." My heart monitor was trying to check out for a refund because my heart rate was so high. I could feel myself tapping into those energy reserves that I usually save for a race. But I thought, "This is it. The last hard one that I'm going to be doing." We came around a turn, and I knew the top had to be there. I was wrong. We had to go around again. The last three or four miles were the hardest I've ever done. By the time we hit the top of the main climb, I felt like a piece of dogmeat.

Fortunately, that was the last intense workout before Hilton Head, and I allowed myself a week off before the race. I knew that I needed to be fairly rested, but if I was too rested, there was a week in between Hilton Head and Hawaii where I could really up my miles again to whatever my body could take. If I was too tired going into Hilton Head, I would have to rest the week after the race, which would be two weeks before Hawaii. That would be too much rest, and the body just slows down. You're not able to store glycogen, and your body starts to lose endurance and speed. The hard part of tapering is finding the balance between resting and keeping the body functions alive, alert, and ready to go.

I really backed off before Hilton Head, and I thought that I was doing a pretty good job of it. I started to lose a bit of my hunger the last week. For me, that's a sure sign of overtraining. If my intake is not equivalent to the amount of miles and effort that I'm putting out, I know that my body is getting tired . . . maybe too tired.

I left for Hilton Head on Friday morning, September 25, on an early-morning flight. I had to be up at 4:00

A.M. to fly to Baltimore, then to Savannah, and finally to do a short drive to Hilton Head. I went to the Kellogg's booth at the prerace expo and signed autographs for an hour or so. Later I was scheduled to do a talk for Schwinn at the carbo-loading dinner. After that, fellow triathlete and sports psychologist, Kirsten Hanssen, and I were scheduled to conduct a training clinic.

The next morning I handed out the awards for a 10K race Kellogg's was sponsoring. After that I got my bike together, had some breakfast, and finally, about 1:30, was able to get out on my bike and see the course. I was feeling a little stressed out over all this. The ideal situation before a race would be for every minute of the day to be my own time. I need quiet time to regroup before a race. The ultimate would be to have somebody buy food, put my bike together, check it, and do everything else that needs to be done. But remember, sports fans, nothing is free. I had to keep reminding myself of that. Still, it's a heck of a lot better to be busy making appearances for your sponsors than to be in your hotel room thinking, "Boy, I wish I was the one who got to go to a booth and sign autographs for people."

I may be whining and screaming and crying and complaining about all I have to do before a race, but I have to continually remind myself that next year I may not be in that position. There might not be a Kellogg's or Schwinn, or Nike . . . maybe not even a sport. I try to keep my energy to myself and just shut up and count my blessings. I know there are at least 1,000 people out there who would love to change places with me, and someday a few of them probably will.

After handing out the awards, I did an ESPN interview and talked to a writer for *Sports Illustrated*. That was a good sign that the sport had finally arrived; *SI* hadn't done a triathlon article since 1983. That year they followed Dave Scott all summer and planned to do a big article on him and how he won the Nice Triathlon. He ended up not winning it (some skinny lifeguard from Del Mar, California, did), and that kind of blew the article. (Sorry about that, *SI*.)

While riding the course, I felt pretty good. I had strength in my legs and a good rhythm, and I felt it would be easy just to roll out there and race. I knew it would be a tough race, because Hilton Head is the National Championship. Some guys forgo Ironman and just key in on this race. I knew that Pigg would be tough because he was really strong that last week or so of training. Pigg was the leader in Coca-Cola Grand Prix points for the season,* and he probably thought it would be nice to win this race so he could win the series on a high note.

The saving grace for me was that the gun went off 1:00 P.M. on Sunday. If it had been a 7:00 or 8:00 A.M. start, I don't know how I would have made it. I hadn't had the time or the sleep I needed to be mentally ready.

When I woke up race morning, the wind was blowing and it was relatively cool, especially for Hilton Head, South

*Coke Grand Prix Rankings. During the Bud Light USTS Season Series (13 races), professional triathletes earn Coke Grand Prix points in each race according to their placings in the top 20, with 100 points for first and 2 for twentieth. Prize money is awarded at the end of the season.

Carolina. I was rested and my body felt really ready. But when the gun went off and we all went in for the swim, I got totally trampled. It was so aggressive I was stunned. I ended up working my way up through the pack. At the pace the leaders were going, it was all I could do to stay with them. I don't mind swimming behind people, because sometimes it's hard for me to lead. I don't have a good sense of pacing. When I'm behind someone, I can keep my pace pretty even.

I was third or so out of the water with a pretty decent lead on Pigg, maybe 20–25 seconds. I hadn't had that much on him in Bermuda or Vancouver. I got on the bike, and up ahead were Rob Mackle and Brooks Clarke. But they weren't too far ahead. I felt a little hot, which might have been from the short-sleeved wet suit I wore in the swim. I started out easy, hoping my body temperature would come down. When it did, I thought, "OK, it's time to start moving up." I went harder and harder and harder, but there was absolutely no change in my speed. That's a good sign your body isn't functioning efficiently. I tried backing off then pushing it, but that didn't work either. I was riding one gear easier than I really should have been. Pigg hadn't caught me yet, but I have that sense and know the pacing of these races. I know what I have to be doing. I was about 5–10 percent slower than I should have been. It took me *forever* to catch those two guys. I just couldn't close any ground. In fact, Mackle was putting time on me.

At about 10 miles, Pigg came by, and he was moving. I thought, "Here's the race. OK, boy you'd better get your ass moving." I stepped on it and was able to pick up the speed a bit. But I was really

"You can have as many of those as you want, Marky." Here I am, Mr. Young and Hip, with my grandma.

maybe two on your plate. Our family hardly ever went to a restaurant, and we didn't have link sausages at home. One time I was camping in the mountains with my grandma. She bought a pack of 84 link sausages and said, "You can have as many of these as you want, Marky!". She started cooking them, and I had one, then five, and finally eight. All of a sudden, I started feeling so damn sick. Just the word *sausage* made me nauseated for weeks. My family would say it just to watch me squirm and turn green. For years after that, I couldn't eat a sausage.

This is known as Mark Allen's Sausage Principle of Triathlons. You love the sport, you love the training, but if you tap into that deep reserve and go too far, your body rejects that pain when you have to do it again.

By the turnaround of the ride, Pigg had 15 seconds on me. I kept telling myself, "Settle down, work through it, work through it." We started back, and Pigg began to put time on me. All of a sudden, I lost contact. In the last 10 miles, he gained a minute and a half. But by the end of the ride, I started to come back, and I caught both Mackle and Clarke.

But could I catch Pigg? I knew his running had improved. In Baltimore, on June 28, I had made up 1 minute and 30 seconds on him in the run. But here I was behind 1 minute and 40 seconds. It was the first run I could remember in which I could not get going. I was flat. It wasn't there. In the back of my mind, I knew I was pretty wasted. I was going as hard as I could go without dipping any further into my reserves. I knew I was in need of some serious recovery time. I thought "Back off. Save it for Hawaii." The leader boards told me I wasn't making any ground on him. I'd

having a tough time. When I had to pick up the pace to match his, the first thought that flashed through my mind was that long last workout going up Golden Gate Canyon. My body was absolutely rejecting that pain threshold I had to reach to maintain contact. You've only got so much physical and emotional energy. If you spread it out, you'll have it at the proper times. But if you tap yourself out, you may not be ready to do it again a week or two later when it's the real thing.

I knew it was going to be really tough to stay with Mike. During some races, your body almost thrives on the pain, that push, that hunger that will not let anyone get away from you. You know you'll do whatever it takes until you drop dead. In other races you start to push, and your body just shuts down.

It's kind of like having a favorite food. When I was a kid, I used to love those little link sausages. When you went to a restaurant, you'd only get gain 5 or 10 seconds, and then he'd make time on me.

Pigg would have been hard to beat even if I was feeling fresh. I was hoping I could hold off Pigg beating me this year, because I was the only top guy he hadn't been able to knock off. It would have been fun to save that for one more season. Pigg needed some incentive to train over the winter, right?

Mentally, winning and losing play a major role when an important race like the Ironman is coming up. You need to maintain confidence in your own strength. You don't want to go into a race like the Ironman feeling de-pressed, fatigued, or down. You need to be positive, recovered, recouped, aggressive, alert, and strong. There is absolutely no room for anything negative. When I was backing off at Hilton Head, I was thinking about the week coming up. I knew we were going to up our mileage once again, depleting ourselves a little further. Before Hilton Head, I couldn't fathom doing another 100-mile ride. I should have been aware that my training had reached a point of diminishing returns. But there is a fine line between being tired and overtired.

10
A FIVE-STICKER RIDE

It is important to be clear about our purposes.
—David K. Reynolds

One day Mike Pigg and I were talking about the upgrade stickers you get from the airlines. If you have so many air miles, you get to fly first class. We were equating our hard efforts with upgrade stickers. One hard effort should be worth one upgrade sticker. We figured, if that was the case, Molina had used all his upgrade stickers from every airline halfway through the year. He was going to be back in economy for a long time.

Personally, I think I used about three of my upgrades climbing those last few miles of Golden Gate Canyon. Hawaii was going to be a five-sticker ride, so I knew I'd better hurry up and find some more.

Minor depression set in after Pigg beat me for the first time and I lost for the first time all year. Still, second place wasn't so bad. After all, if Pigg

hadn't been in there, I would have been hero for a day.

Back home in Colorado, I rationalized the whole thing. I decided it was better that I had lost. If I had barely won, I might not have noticed how tired I was. I'd have been so excited from the victory that I wouldn't have been able to assess my body's needs efficiently. Instead, I knew what I had to do for Hawaii. I needed to rest. I had to do a long ride, maybe two, and a long run. But no more junk miles! I had to rest and focus my energies on myself.

Before the Ironman, I had an intense dream. I was out at Torrey Pines State Beach in Del Mar, trying to go surfing. In my dreams, being out in surf is always significant, symbolic of power and energy. In this dream, I was trying to paddle out through the whitewater, attempting to reach where the surf was breaking. Other people were surfing. They'd get three-quarters of the way out, and they'd lose their boards. I'd paddle over and retrieve their boards for them. I'd start to get washed in, and then someone else would have problems. I'd go help that person, too. I realized I wasn't able to get myself out to the zone of power. I was getting sucked down the beach and losing my way.

After I woke up, it was clear to me what that dream meant. I realized that for the preceding five weeks, a lot of energy had been going out to people I was training with. I would say little things to pump them up, to keep them psyched and feeling good about what they were doing. We all need each other to get through some of those workouts. Training is such a mutual thing. But it was time for me to stop giving away my energy. I knew it wasn't going to be easy to do, because I enjoy encouraging others, working together toward a goal. But now all my energy had to go directly to Mark Allen. It was time to go into a shell, to do my own thing. I had to absolutely and totally respond to the exact workouts I needed to do, when I needed to do them.

It was tough, because I didn't want Pigg to think I had sour grapes because he beat me at Hilton Head. It would be very easy for Mike to interpret my actions that way. I did the best I could to maintain a neutral relationship with everyone without looking like a jerk, or like someone suffering from a severe case of jealousy.

I started to get on the Mark Allen schedule, into the Mark Allen routine. The last long ride I took was on a Tuesday, and during the last five to ten miles of it, my knee really started to hurt. That worried me. My body was telling me that I had better back off. The next morning when I woke up, I didn't know if I'd even be able to do Hawaii.

I knew a visit to the local witch doctor was in order. By the next morning, my knee was taken care of, and all of a sudden everything started feeling really good. My workouts were easier, and I was under total control. The work was starting to require less and less effort.

Finally, I could feel that my body had absorbed strength from the long series of hard workouts before Hilton Head. It felt so good. I thought, "Things are starting to come together."

I knew I was finally in balance when the article on Hilton Head came out in *Sports Illustrated*. There was a big picture of Pigg on the bike and another of Kirsten Hanssen. My first reaction was "All right! That's great!" I was excited that *SI* decided to do a triathlon and Pigg finally got some major press. I didn't feel jealous about the article at all. I know you can't have everything in your sport all the time. You've got to share the spotlight with other people. I try to stand outside myself as much as I can and evaluate my reactions to situations. When I'm really emotional about something, I'll say, "OK, where is that emotion coming from? Why is it different this time? Put another check in the positive list and know that you are on the right track here."

If the same thing had happened a week or two earlier, it would have blown my mind for a day or two because I hadn't maintained or contained my own strength, my own power. When you're maintaining power within

It's important to remember exactly what you have to do when you get into the transition area. It's easy to get flustered, especially if some guy is pointing a camera in your face. You should know beforehand which direction you'll be leaving from. One of my most embarrassing moments came in a transition area. I rode into the wrong area and tried to put someone else's running shoes on. They were too small, but I thought the problem was that my feet had swollen during the bike ride. Eventually, I found my own shoes.

Photo courtesy of Bud Light USTS

yourself, the whole world could go into a tizzy, and you wouldn't budge. But once you start moving away, lose that center, someone could blow on you and you'd fall over.

I was almost packed, except for my bike, and I had all the food and goodies I needed to take over Hawaii. My clothes were washed and the apartment picked up far in advance. Everything was coming together, and I could feel my personal power bubbling to the surface.

What is this personal power that I talk about? Imagine you're standing on a huge plate 25 feet in diameter, balanced on a tiny fulcrum. The center is your power spot, your axis. It's difficult for people to knock you off of that, but once you step away from the center, you'll have a hard time staying balanced. If you get too far out to the side, no one even has to be around; you'll fall off by yourself.

You can give your power away to other people, so be careful. In 1986, Scott Tinley was not at the center of his strength when it came to Hawaii. He was having a fairly difficult time with all the pressure, and he was feeling frazzled. He had had a hard season in which he had overtrained and overraced. When he heard that Mark Allen had decided to do the Ironman, it threw him into a tailspin. He was not at his center of power, and when he heard I was racing, he gave up a lot of his power. It was the first (and last) time I'd ever seen Tinley do that.

When I arrived in Kona that year, I went out around sunset one evening to do a swim at the pier. Tinley and Murphy Reinschreiber came swimming to the beach. Murphy swam over to me, but Tinley was so out of whack with himself that he swam underwater to try to avoid talking to me. When he finally came up, I said, "Scott, how's it going?" He just nodded his head. He wouldn't even speak to me! And I thought, "This is *Scott Tinley*?!" In the past, he'd been better than anyone at

keeping his focus and power within himself. He never before gave that up to other people.

In 1987 everyone said Dave Scott would go Nice instead of the Ironman. Then there was a big announcement in Bermuda that Dave wasn't going to Nice after all, he was going to Hawaii. All season I thought Dave wasn't going to be in Hawaii, but I wanted to have the race, the fitness and mental attitude so that if he were there, I could beat him. When I heard he was going to Hawaii, I thought "Shit, the guy is really going to be there!" I realized it hadn't been just a mental exercise. It made a big difference in the way I trained.

I saw him in the hotel lobby in Bermuda and said, "I hear you're going to the Ironman." "Yeah," he said, "I've decided to go back." At that moment, I gave some of my power over to him. I could feel it going from me to him. I was so aware of it, I thought, "I've got to get that back, I can't let that sucker go into the race with my power in his pocket."

There are many examples of athletes using this kind of power game to their advantage. Moments before the swimming finals of the 1964 Olympics, gold medalist Don Schollander followed his main opponent into the bathroom and stood behind him while he tried to take a leak. There were maybe 100 urinals in there and the guy became so frustrated and upset that he couldn't get on with it, and ran out. You could say the guy was totally psyched out by Don—that he gave Don all his power. *That's* when Don Schollander won the gold medal.

11
IRONWEEK

Whether you remember or anticipate, you do
it now.

—David K. Reynolds

On Thursday, October 1, just over a week before the Ironman, Julie Moss and I flew into Kona. We used our upgrade stickers and got to hang out in first class. We ate some decent food, stretched out, and relaxed.

I remember what it was like when we got off the plane. We'd spent the summer in Colorado, and we had a couple of weeks of cold and rainy weather, but the last two weeks before I left were 75 and 80 degrees every day. I got off the plane in Kona, and it felt like someone had opened a hot oven door. "My God," I thought, "I'm not used to this kind of heat." I said to Julie, "If this were race day, I don't know how people would make it." It was incredibly hot. We found out from the locals that there had been a heat wave for the last month. I felt a little bit better that it wasn't just me being oversensitive. It really *was* hot.

Mike Pigg was coming in on Saturday and wanted to ride the course or at least do a long ride with me on Sunday. I said if I felt good on Saturday I'd do the ride then, so he'd be on his own. Saturday I woke up feeling fine, so I rode along at my own pace and stopped when I wanted to. Even though it would have been nice to have had some company, I needed to work out alone to keep myself within myself and not respond, or give out energy, or interact with my main competition in this race.

I felt like I had all the time in the world before this race, especially in comparison to Hilton Head, where I had had no time at all to myself. I had over a week, and had already done my last really long ride. My biggest worry was what to eat for my next meal.

Resting is interesting, because you've done all your workouts and (hopefully) you've become strong from them.

That's also when you think about the competition. I knew Dave Scott, not to mention Tinley and Pigg, would be totally ready. There would be two or three other guys, Europeans or Australians, that I hadn't counted on who I knew would have a great race.

Whatever happened out there, I wanted my body to be in shape to put out that supreme mental and physical effort. As each day went by, there were moments when I knew my body was really getting strong. It had the reserve I would need when things got tough out there. I knew I'd be able to push through anything.

I kept one particular image in my mind. A few years ago I saw two great cyclists, Greg Lemond and Bernand Hinault, compete in the Coors Classic. Watching those guys on bikes was incredible. While all the other cyclists looked like they were really hurting, Hinault and Lemond were so efficient on their bikes they looked as if they could break away at any time. Keeping up with the pack wasn't a 110 percent effort for them. Before the race, I had that image of myself on the bike, being able to spin my way along, no matter what the pace or who was there.

I devised a little bit of a race strategy. I tried to picture how things would feel and be during the race. I knew I'd be even with Dave during the swim. That's one thing he's very consistent about, and, whether I try to or not, I always end up coming out of the water at the same time he does.

In a race like Hawaii, it's important to keep an eye on the competition during the swim, because, with the ABC vans out there, if someone comes out of the water 30 seconds or a minute ahead, you may be able to see him on

the bike and still not be able to close the gap. The cars get backed up in front of the leader, and when the camera zooms in for a close-up shot for 15 or 30 seconds, the leader gets a draft and immediately gains some time. In the bike, it's vital to maintain close contact from the start.

The swim didn't seem like it should be an important part of the day, not something that was going to be hard or easy. I felt no anxiety about the swim. But every time I thought about the bike, I felt Pigg would really try to go hard.

Pigg had had a great cycling season. He would probably figure that some of the guys could run him down in the marathon. If he were going to win the race, he'd need to put some time on them in the bike. I had an image of him and me neck and neck on the bike, putting 5 or 10 minutes on the rest of the field.

I didn't know where Dave would be on the bike. He hadn't ridden well all year. At times, he is really strong on the bike, but he hadn't shown any of that strength in the year's shorter races. Who could know what he would be like? If he was with me and holding a really good pace, I wasn't going to be an idiot and blow myself out like I did in 1984. If I was with him in the beginning and his pace was slow, though, I wasn't going to be afraid to pull away.

Next I thought about the run. There is a part of me that feels, "If I'm with Dave off the bike, I can run with him this year." I didn't have the fear of the marathon I'd had in the past, that sense of unknowing, of "My God, what is going to happen in 26 miles out there?"

I've felt terrible off the bike, and I've felt like death off the bike. I've never felt *good* off the bike in Hawaii. The first six miles of the run seem to be my undoing. Nevertheless, I thought that once I made it to the turnaround, I'd be OK. I've never run slower from the turnaround back than from five miles out to the turnaround. If I were walking at that point, I'd at least be doing that, if not better, at the end. If I were running, so much the better. Once I hit the turnaround, I usually run even faster.

I felt really strong in my mind, my energy, my body. I knew I had the ability to do that run pretty well. Dave and Tinley predicted that a 2:40 marathon was possible if the conditions were right. I thought about it, but 2:40 seemed pretty damn fast to me—not out of the question, but it would have to be the right type of day to run 2:40 in Hawaii. The way the weather was going, it just didn't seem reasonable.

I guess I also felt some fear. I always have those question marks. I mean, what if I give it all I can, and somebody just blows by me and I can't stay with it? If that happens, it happens. On the Ironman course, you can't force anything. You definitely can't force a pace that is unrealistic for you. You have to respect that race the whole way and be ready for the worst. The worst that could ever happen would be to be outraced. The best would be to outrace everyone else. Before a race, I have never expected I would have to walk on the marathon. After six years in the sport I'd done the race five times, finishing four times. I'd done long workouts and trained in the heat. I knew what it feels like when the body starts to go downhill, and I knew what to do in case that ever happened.

When I think of being outraced, I try

It's race time! I'm getting everything ready that I will need during the bike ride. In a few minutes, I'll be in the Kailua-Kona harbor.
Photo by Bob Babbitt

to do two things. One is never to give away my power. When that happens, in my mind I've become a little weak. In a sense, it's giving up. The second thing is to maintain my balance, my strength, no matter what happens. That's the attitude I need to race with. If I maintain myself within the center of my strength, there's no predicting what will happen between that point and the finish line. I may be 15 miles out and really have to slow down and let someone go by. If I sacrifice my internal self at that moment, that person is going to win the race. So, no matter who goes by me, I don't give up. He could always fall apart later, and I could end up winning.

It's a crapshoot out there. I know my feelings during any situation in a race, when I'm in the best place I can be. Ninety-nine percent of the time when I'm thinking about the race before it, I feel 100 percent strong and 100 percent positive. There are very few doubts in my mind. When I have doubts, I tend to play them out. I find that spot within myself where I know what it feels like to be 100 percent of what I could be in a 50 percent situation.

Every now and then, I thought about my performance in Hawaii in relation to sponsorship. I do the Kellogg's Pro Grain commercial. They were banking that after October 10, 1987, they would have the winner of the Ironman endorsing the official Ironman food. If you sponsor someone and he turns out to win the gold medal, you've got a pretty valuable commodity. If he gets second place, it doesn't mean much.

The question in my mind was what would happen if I didn't win the race? Was it going to affect my relationship with Kellogg's? Would they bail out on me? Would they bail out on the cereal? Would they use me the next year? Or would they use Dave Scott or Scott Tinley? The same goes for my other sponsors. I'm sure Nike and Schwinn had some things on their drawing board, and thought, "Let's see if Mark is able to win the Ironman. We can do this and this and this if he does."

I have the title "the five-time world champion" because of my wins in Nice.

But look at the way people are introduced at the races. "Here is Scott Molina, who hasn't been having that good a year this time around." He gets second, he gets fifth, but no matter where he finishes, he's always ahead of Tinley. Yet when Tinley gets introduced, it's always, "Here's Scott Tinley, the only man to beat Dave Scott at the Ironman." It's a calling card.

Winning Ironman is not the end-all, obviously. Even though I had never won the race, I didn't feel like I had suffered because of it. I had carved my niche from other races. Win, lose, or draw, that would continue. Still, sponsorship, endorsement, and credibility would sure be a lot easier if I could win it. I think a lot of people hoped Mark Allen could win it. An equal or greater number hoped Dave Scott would win it for the sixth time, that Tinley would pull it out, or that Mike Pigg would upset all the big boys and show he's one tough cookie.

Thoughts like these didn't give me a lot of strength. You race because of motivation, and I knew I needed something more. For me, a monetary reward or an increase in credibility and stature in other people's minds is great, but that can't be my ultimate goal. When I've lost big races, my disappointment has been that I didn't do what I set out to do, that my performance wasn't what it could have been. Later I might think, "I can't believe the amount of money I would have won if I'd won that whole thing!" But that's always secondary. Of course, the economic facts of life are part of living in the real world. The compensation can be great, and sure, money is a major motivating factor. But making money is not my ultimate goal in life.

When I'm lying on my deathbed, I want to feel as if I did the best I could do. I didn't back off, I followed through on what I wanted to do. And out of everything I did, I could feel that I had a positive influence on some people. I didn't just suck things in, I gave back out.

Maybe my motivation in this race would be the need to beat Dave Scott, Scott Tinley, or Mike Pigg. To focus on beating a particular rival means I have to be alert and aware of him throughout the entire race. In other words, his race has to interact with mine.

The best scenario is to use your opponents' pace, respond to their strategy, and do it in a mechanical, noninteractive way. If someone says, "Can you rub my neck?" you could do it in a mechanical way, and they'll feel as if you hadn't done a thing for them. Or you can rub their neck and put yourself into it and be totally interactive with them. It's the same with racing. If you get too emotionally involved with the other people in that race, it can suck energy out of you and you could get off center. Then you start doing someone else's race.

None of this is absolute, however. The whole purpose of competing is to beat other people, to win your race. They try to beat you, and you try to beat them. If there is no interaction during the race, we'd all be going at training speed. That's why I race, to go as fast as I can.

So when I'm not feeling good or when the negative thoughts start creeping into my mind, how do I insulate myself from that? I like to imagine that I'm racing inside a big, long cathedral corridor that extends over me in all directions. It's invisible, but it has a magnetic energy around it that is all mine. Any energy that leaves my body goes up into the cathedral structure and focuses back into me. I have no interaction with the other athletes. It gives me strength just thinking about it. When I imagine this before the race, my legs almost tingle. I can feel this energy coming into my body.

A couple of days before the race, I thought, "I've got three days to just carbo-load to the max here." I'd been trying to be careful, because when you cut back your workouts, your body's needs are also reduced. I was not expending much energy. Tuesday, I did a moderately long swim, a 45-mile bike, and a 4-mile run. When you're resting, you need to balance out the rest. That includes depleting your body enough so it will store up for the race. It's important to rest but not to let your body functions slow down too much. As I rest, sleep, and relax, I consciously tell my body that it has to be ready to race, that it has to maintain sharpness and strength. When most people rest, everything slows down too much. They go into a race, and they're told to rest and taper. They do, but their body has slowed down 5–10 percent and they start to feel sluggish. Make a conscious note to keep that little bit of tension in your body even though it's time to store up. You want just enough tension so you're ready to go on race day. The goal is to be strong and alert and not to have to give the body a full-on kick start come race morning.

Wednesday night before the race, I decided, "This is it, my last good night of relaxing, the last day without things to do." Thursday I had a pro meeting and had to check in my clothes. Friday was the bike check. I wanted to get this thing done with! I wanted to make sure my body wasn't ready one day too

Before the race, I check out the strap, my Ironday advantage. My agent, Charlie Graves, gives me a final pep talk.
Photo by Bob Babbitt

early, that on race day I wouldn't be one day beyond my peak. I was ready. I wanted to do that race. All the anticipation, the prerace workouts, and the thinking about it were getting old.

Thursday morning was the pro meeting, and everyone was there. It was the first time Dave, Tinley, Pigg, and I had been together all week. I could feel the tension in that room. We were in a tiny hotel room, discussing drafting on the bike course. Every top triathlete in the world was in that room with one goal in mind: to have the most outrageous race he or she could have.

When I sat down on the floor, I was looking directly at Dave. He was sitting sideways, looking away from me. He knew I was there, but he never once looked at me. It was the first time I felt like he, Tinley, and I were total equals on this course. Usually Hawaii is thought of as Dave's domain. After all, he's won the thing five times. He's the warrior in his own country. You're not competing on neutral ground in Hawaii.

This was the first time I didn't feel intimidated by the competition. Win, lose, or draw, we started out on equal footing. Being the underdog can have its advantages, but I'd rather be a clear-cut favorite.

12
IRONDAY, PART 1

Self-confidence comes after accomplishment,
not before.

—David K. Reynolds

My bike mechanic, Steve Hed, gave me a strap to clip onto the stem of my bike. The strap keeps you in an aerodynamic position and all your strength goes directly into the pedaling. So then, of course, you go faster. Apparently, the Italians used it during the team time trials at the World Championships this past summer. They had great success, beating the Russians. Steve told me to use it, but to keep it out of sight. He gave it to me just two days before I turned in my bike. I tried it out on Friday morning, riding the hills, the flats, and into the wind. I couldn't tell if it was helping, not helping, or cutting into my legs and shutting off my blood supply.

While I was testing the strap on the high road, away from the crowds, Steve Hed drove by. He stopped, we chatted, and he adjusted the belt. I looked up the road and saw a long line of cyclists heading our way. I didn't want any of the top guys to see me with the strap. As the cyclists got closer, I was thinking, "Jeez, these guys are going to see this thing, but who the heck is going to be coming down this hill on Friday, the day before the race?" As they got closer, I recognized Pigg and a bunch of his friends. I turned sideways and hoped they wouldn't stop. I thought, "Pigg's gonna see the belt, and he's gonna get one, too."

I didn't know if the thing would work or not, but if you show up on the race course with some funky new device, it's bound to blow their minds. Pigg slowed down. "Just checking out the new machinery," he said. Then he smiled and continued on. I thought he'd stop and say, "Mark, what *is* that you've got on?" That's all I needed. All the top guys showing up race morning wearing *my* prerace advantage.

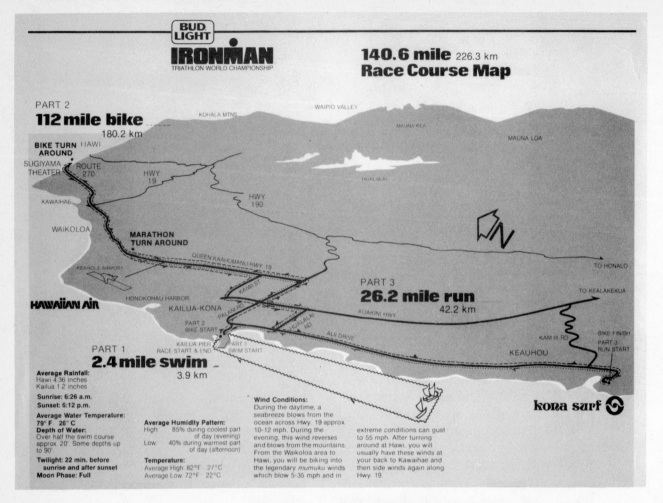

BUD LIGHT
IRONMAN
TRIATHLON WORLD CHAMPIONSHIP

140.6 mile 226.3 km
Race Course Map

PART 2
112 mile bike
180.2 km

BIKE TURN AROUND HAWI
SUGIYAMA THEATER — ROUTE 270

KOHALA MTNS.
WAIPIO VALLEY
MAUNA KEA
MAUNA LOA
KAWAIHAE
HWY 19
HWY 190
HUALALAI
WAIKOLOA

MARATHON TURN AROUND
QUEEN KAAHUMANU HWY 19
KEAHOLE AIRPORT
N
TO HONALO

HAWAIIAN AIR

HONOKOHAU HARBOR
KAILUA-KONA
PART 2 BIKE START
KAILUA PIER RACE START & END
PALANI RD.
KAIWI ST.
PART 1 SWIM START
HUALALAI RD.
ALII DRIVE

PART 3
26.2 mile run
42.2 km

KUAKINI HWY
TO KEALAKEKUA
KAM III RD.
KEAUHOU
BIKE FINISH
PART 3 RUN START

PART 1
2.4 mile swim
3.9 km

kona surf

Average Rainfall:
Hawi 4.36 inches
Kailua 1.2 inches

Sunrise: 6:26 a.m.
Sunset: 6:12 p.m.

Average Water Temperature:
79°F 26°C
Depth of Water:
Over half the swim course
approx. 20'. Some depths up
to 90'.

Twilight: 22 min. before
sunrise and after sunset
Moon Phase: Full

Average Humidity Pattern:
High: 85% during coolest part
   of day (evening)
Low: 40% during warmest part
   of day (afternoon)

Temperature:
Average High: 82°F 27°C
Average Low: 72°F 22°C

Wind Conditions:
During the daytime, a
seabreeze blows from the
ocean across Hwy. 19 approx.
10-12 mph. During the
evening, this wind reverses
and blows from the mountains.
From the Waikoloa area to
Hawi, you will be biking into
the legendary *mumuku* winds
which blow 5-35 mph and in
extreme conditions can gust
to 55 mph. After turning
around at Hawi, you will
usually have these winds at
your back to Kawaihae and
then side winds again along
Hwy. 19.

This is the Ironman Triathlon course as it looks on paper. Racing it, however, is an entirely different story.
Map courtesy of Bud Light Ironman

On Wednesday, three days before the Ironman, before I even knew about my new cycling toy, I began to load up for the race. I never, ever had a problem eating before Ironman, but this year every time I ate, I got full really quickly. Julie Moss and I were eating all our meals together, and she was putting away more food than I was. I was eating half of what I normally would. Then after each meal I'd start to feel sick, like I was going to throw up. I thought, "Maybe I'm a little nervous, or maybe my body is just ready to go and doesn't need all this food."

Sometimes if you eat a lot, you get tired and sleepy. It's just too much for your body to digest. On the other hand, the last thing you want on race day is to bonk, to run out of energy, because you didn't eat enough. Walking the marathon can make for a long day out there.

I didn't pay much attention to my eating. I did notice it, though, and so did Julie. We went to the Aloha Cafe Friday morning to fill up on French toast and pancakes. I had three-quarters of a piece of French toast, and that was it. Again I felt nauseated. "Well," I thought, "Just keep confident. Maybe this is my body's way of telling me not to overdo it now because I'll have to overdo it tomorrow." I felt set.

For lunch on Friday, Julie and I had a big veggie meal at Amy's Cafe. Again, I couldn't eat much. I barely got through one plateful at an all-you-can-eat place, and I felt gross. But my confidence was still together. It didn't faze me.

Later, I shaved down and had a quick leg rub. I got my bike together and took it to the pier to check it in. I went for a final spin, and my body and my legs felt good. I ran into George Hoover at the bike check. It was great to see him. We looked at each other, and I thought about everything we'd been through in the sport together. A lot can be said in about five seconds of looking at someone. We've both had our share of disappointments in Hawaii. He's done the Ironman a few times and has always cramped up and fallen apart during the run. The last time, he had to go to the hospital when his body went into a total spasm.

I think we both knew it was time to have a good one, time to erase those old memories. We went out and rode a couple of miles with each other and just talked about a whole lot of nothing.

I came back to the pier and noticed that Dave's bike was sitting in a pickup truck away from all the rest. It was in a bike rack in the bed of the truck, and someone was standing there admiring it. I thought it was ironic. Everyone else was checking their bikes in, and his was sitting up in this truck bed all by itself.

Tinley's bike was hilarious. He had already checked it in. He had a doll hanging from a noose on his handle

Here's a good look at my race advantage. It's a strap called a "Seat Leash," that went around my waist and attached to the stem of the bike. The Italians had great success using it at the world championships earlier in the year.
Photo by Lois Schwartz

bars. It was a little naked girl doll that had "Dave Scott" printed on the front. Just seeing that doll broke all the tension for me.

When I got to the pier, all the triathletes were wishing each other good luck. Everyone was nervous, no matter who he was. When I checked in my bike, people zoomed in on it to see what equipment I had. I have a Schwinn with Scott DH bars and Shimano components. It's really basic, something anyone and his brother could have for a decent price. You can't go out and buy a fast bicycle. What makes a bike fast is not the trick components, it's your legs, your heart, and your mind. That's what makes a bike fly.

The final Ironman prerace ritual is turning your bike in. After that, I started to think about Dave. We had had an interesting encounter a few days earlier. Julie had to do an ABC interview, so I decided to go to the Nike booth in the Kona Surf Hotel for a while. Afterward, I went back over to where the interviews were taking place, because I thought Julie might still be there. Mike Pigg was waiting to do his interview. Dave had just sat down, and he was sitting there under the bright lights. They hadn't asked him any questions yet, because they were adjusting his microphone. While I stood there watching him, I remembered back to 1986. I had gone out for an evening swim at the pier. Dave and his wife, Anna, were just finishing up their swim. Dave congratulated me on winning Nice and asked me how I was planning to do at Ironman. It was a neat exchange.

The 1987 season was different. I can't say if it was Dave or me, but our relationship felt totally different. I felt a little more apprehensive. There was more pressure. Last year, people were saying, "Dave won, but Mark won Nice two weeks beforehand. Who knows what might have happened if he had been fresh?"

I don't like that kind of conjecture, because it takes away from someone else's performance. Dave had an outstanding race. Maybe he was thinking that if I was fresh this time, I might beat him. Dave's got a lot of confidence in himself, but things can change a lot in a year.

Since October 1986, the Kellogg's Pro Grain commercials have helped my recognizability and credibility. Add to that a great year of racing, and all of

a sudden Ironman was no longer just the Dave Scott Show . . . there were other players in the game.

I walked up to where they were doing the interview with Dave. I was looking at him, but I wasn't really thinking about anything. He glanced over, and his eye caught mine. I don't know if he was aware of it or not, but his whole face tightened up. Five or ten minutes later, I replayed the scene in my mind, and I realized that at that moment, he had given up a little bit of his power. That surprised me, because Dave is one of those guys who rarely gives up his power.

The interview was the first time I had seen Pigg before the race. He didn't have the same aura around him that he has at the USTS races. Those are his babies, and he knows how to race them. I had a sense that he knew he would have to respect this course, that he couldn't race the Ironman the same as a USTS event. I was glad to be able to tell Pigg face-to-face that I hoped he had a great day. I hadn't made any contact with him the whole week before, because I needed to do my own thing.

By Friday night I did all my visualization. I had it clear in my mind what I wanted to eat, when I needed to drink, and how everything was going to work. I was hoping for a good race, not only for me, but for my parents, who were there. I knew my friends back home were rooting for me, too. Having a great performance is a way of paying back the people who have always supported you. People put an incredible amount of energy into me during the period before the race. They give up a lot of themselves to make everything work for me. I have to become self-focused to have the race of my life. That

So you want to do the Ironman? Well, the day begins with 1,500 swimmers all trying to get out of the bay in tiny Kailua-Kona at the same time. After 2.4 miles, you get a chance to go for a bike ride.
Photo courtesy of Bud Light Ironman

requires people to help you out and do things that they normally wouldn't.

My night of sleep on Friday wasn't too bad, all things considered. I had a dream that I missed the swim start and started the race 45 minutes behind everyone else. "I'm never going to make up all that time," I thought. In my dream, I started the swim just when the last guys were about to finish. The race organizers let me go anyway. I always have at least one of those dreams before a race.

The alarm went off race morning at 5:00. I woke up easily. My first thought was, "What am I going to have to do today?"

I felt like everything was going along pretty well. My theory is that if I urinate too much the day before a race, I've carbo-loaded too early and am releasing the stored glycogen too soon. This time I felt I had loaded up just enough. I wasn't too hungry when I woke up, but I had a little bit to eat anyway. I noticed that I was really tight around my diaphragm. It didn't make sense. I never get tight there.

Warming up for the swim, just stretching out flat in the water, really pulled something in my stomach. I tried to loosen it up, but nothing seemed to work. My stomach doesn't usually get tight or upset before a race. I've been competing for so long that I can relax my stomach even when I'm really nervous. It didn't make sense.

When I left the condo, I could see that it was an absolutely clear day. You could see all the mountains in the distance. At the pier, people were finally realizing what they were going to have to do out there, what they were in for. When you look in their eyes, you can tell that they're thinking, "What have I gotten myself into?"

When you've done that race more than once, there is a part of you that accepts the fact that anything can happen to you out there. It's kind of a peaceful feeling, knowing that it's going to be a long and intense day. I knew that no matter how much I prepared, at some point during the day things would get tough. It could be something as simple as missing a food or water pass at an aid station. You can get flustered because you needed water at that moment and it's going to be hard to get to the next aid station without it. I knew I'd live through a lifetime of emotions and experiences in the course of one day.

The only thing I can begin to compare Ironman to is the Med CATs. That was a full day of total concentration. Ironman demands total mental concentration, but you also must perform physical movement for a long period of time. No inch of your body will escape the stress of the Ironman.

George Hoover and I swam out and loosened up together. I lined up at the start. For some reason, I always end up close to Dave. I guess I have to admit, it's intentional; it's important for me to keep an eye on the guy. I knew the swim would be different this year because the Hinshaws, Chris and Brad, weren't racing this year. They were usually the first guys out of the water, and there was always a gap between the Hinshaws and the rest of us. Since they weren't in the race, I felt confident that I would be fairly close to the front this year. I was 10th or 15th out of the water in 1986.

The start wasn't too bad—which meant I didn't get kicked or jostled, and I still had all my teeth. A swim start with 1,500 people is sort of like spending a few hours in a roller derby. Arms and legs come flying at you from every imaginable direction. I noticed Dave in front of me, and I thought, "OK, I'll just hang with him during this part of the swim." He took off at the gun, and I couldn't believe how fast he went for the first 500 yards! Definitely faster than he goes in a USTS event. I knew I couldn't let him go.

A few years ago, in 1983, I thought he was behind me in the swim, but he was actually up ahead. He ended up with a 1½-minute lead. Then he got on the bike and took off. By the time I found out that he was ahead, he had picked up another minute on the bike. At the turnaround, 55 miles out, he was seven minutes ahead and the race was over.

I knew I had to come out of the water with the guy. I took the turn at the halfway boat and saw Dave backstroke for a stroke or two to see who was on his feet. I know it bugs the *hell* out of him when I'm on his feet, but that's part of the game. Two guys were on my feet—since it's legal to draft in the swim, everyone is looking for a fast pair of feet to swim behind.

Finally, the pace started to slow down to something more reasonable for a 50-minute, 2.4-mile swim. I had time to rest and catch my breath. If Dave had kept up that pace the whole

Ironday: Coming out of the 2.4-mile swim, I was just behind Dave Scott and just in front of Mike Pigg.
Photo by Lois Schwartz

way, it would have been a tough swim.

When we came out of the water, only a few swimmers were ahead of Dave and me. Two guys behind me sprinted the last few hundred yards as we came in. I pulled those guys through the swim, then they tried to pick up the prime for finishing first, second, or third out of the water. It's kind of a cheap shot, but that's also part of the game. To me, it wasn't worth it. What's a couple of hundred dollars if the final sprint puts you into oxygen debt? You can't afford to get on the bike and start out too slow.

Dave and I raced up the ramp together. I went into the change tent to do my strip number and put on my cycling gear. The idea is to be fast, not modest. I ran over to my bike and threw my jam sandwiches into the pocket of my jersey. When you throw on a cycling jersey while you're wet, the thing just rolls up on itself. But in order to get the pocket open, you have to be able to pull it all the way down so you can put your food in there. It's so agonizingly slow. It probably takes all of 15 seconds to pull it all the way down, but it seems like an eternity. In a short race where I don't carry food, I just throw the jersey on, and eventually it comes down on its own. Finally, after squirming and wiggling for a while, the pocket opened up and my jam sandwiches had a home.

I hopped on my bike and started out from the transition area. Dave had his shoes already attached to his pedals, and I'd never seen him do that before. I figured he might not be totally adept at putting his shoes on while he was moving. On the other hand, I wasn't quite used to tightening the Velcro strap on my new Nike cycling shoes. The two of us left the transition area, both intent on getting it together before going up the first hill out of town. It's impossible to make it up that hill without your shoes on.

I stepped into my Shimano pedals, but I couldn't get my feet in tight because I couldn't get a hold of the Velcro strap. Dave was next to me and was having problems getting his feet into

See what happened when Mike Pigg put on his cycling jersey when he was wet? It just sat there, a large lump in the middle of his back. That's OK when you're doing a triathlon with a 25-mile bike ride and don't have to use the jersey pocket for food. But in a long-distance race like Ironman, that pocket is crucial.
Photo by C. J. Olivares, Jr.

In this photo, Pigg is to my left. I like to use the other athletes to help monitor my own pace, but I don't like my race to be too tied to someone else's.
Photo by Lois Schwartz

his shoes. Both of us were looking down, and the next thing I knew we were both heading right toward each other in a sort of slow-motion cycling ballet. We hit shoulders, and I swear I thought both of us were going down. I could hear the crowd. Half of them were shrieking, "Watch out! Ooooh, ooooh, oh no!" The other half were laughing. I couldn't believe it. I felt like saying, "Hey, you can get your jollies somewhere else . . . we're having some problems here!" We were all of 10 seconds into the bike ride.

At the base of the first hill, someone went by me on a Basso. My mind was totally alert, taking note of everything that was going on. One minute went by before it clicked. "One guy went by . . . who was that, Tom Gallagher? No, it's Pigg. OK, there's Pigg . . . where's Dave? He's right there in front of me." The pace was moderate at the beginning. We all looked around and saw each other, but no one was willing to take the lead and go for it. All of a sudden, I thought, "Are we going to have a 112-mile cat-and-mouse game?" A lot of times, those first 25 miles can be pretty fast. But this race was starting to look like a blueprint of last year's ride where I hung with Dave because I knew that my body wasn't totally recovered from Nice.

I just sat back for a little bit, wondering how Pigg was riding, what the pace was like, whether Pigg was going to be really aggressive. If he went off the front, my plan was to stick with him. If

1984 and self-destructed on the run. Unless I felt I could go by them and pull away, I didn't want to make the attempt. Plus, I didn't want Dave to see my harness just yet. I wanted to keep that to myself. At that point, I wasn't even sure it was going to work.

The strap had two screw attachments that can be loosened or tightened as you go. Suddenly they came unscrewed from the fixture, and everything started clinking and clanking. I had to sit up and get it all back together again.

Near the airport, my nose started to bleed. I don't know why it happened. I didn't breathe hard or smack it during the swim. I tried wiping my nose, and

Below: I watched Dave Scott very carefully during the early part of the bike ride. I wanted to make sure he didn't get too far off the front.
Photo by Lois Schwartz

Above: Everyone expected Mike Pigg to try to get away during the bike. If he did, I planned to go with him. He seemed content to stay in the pack.
Photo by Lois Schwartz

we could put 5–10 minutes on the field, that would be a major advantage going into the run. It's hard for someone to make up that kind of time on you.

It didn't pan out that way. Pigg went to the front several times, but it wasn't a blazing, blistering pace. It was fast enough, though. My thoughts were, "Hey, I don't want to go any faster. It's early in the bike, and I've been the hero out in front before!" I came in 12 minutes ahead of everyone off the bike in my hand was soon covered with blood. I flagged down a marshall and said, "You've got to get me some Kleenex, something to put in my nose." I pulled up next to Pigg to show him. This had happened once or twice during our training rides. Pigg looked over at me and shook his head in disbelief.

Finally, the medical van came up, and someone handed me a piece of gauze to shove up my nose. I was already a quart low. I had to ride holding my handle bars with one hand and my nose with the other. "OK, just go with it," I thought. "It's early in the race; there's nothing to get upset about." I left the gauze in for the first 40 miles. I'm sure I looked pretty handsome with this big old piece of bloody gauze hanging out of my nose. I thought, "Hey, it's a party out here. You've got to come dressed for the occasion."

Nothing eventful was happening. We were putting in the miles, going through the motions, the lead changing a few times here and there. I felt Tinley was going to catch us at some point, because I knew the pace was too slow to stay ahead of the guy. Tinley's no dummy. He knew that he had to catch us early in the bike, before the turn-around, because otherwise it would be hard to make up any ground. We'd be out of sight, out of mind.

Other riders started to catch us. Keith Anderson from South Africa was the first. This was the Ironman, we're talking the Ironman Triathlon, and Anderson went by wearing a Speedo. That's it. I thought to myself, "Man, the sun is really, really hot. I don't care who you are, you're going to be fried if you're out here for over eight hours with no shirt on. Especially on the bike when your back is totally exposed to

It's hard to tell in the photo, but my nose had already started to bleed. This was the beginning of a long day in the lava fields.
Photo by Lois Schwartz

the sun." I also thought about how my groin would be screaming if I rode 112 miles in a Speedo. That's not a pleasant thought.

When Anderson, Mr. Screaming Groin, went by, he was going a pretty decent pace. It was starting to look more like a bike race out there. It's kind of funny how the sport has evolved into

Above: Just after Hawi, 55 miles out, Ken Glah from Westchester, Pennsylvania, went blasting by us. He led all the way to the 80-mile mark.
Photo by Lois Schwartz

we started the climb up toward Hawi. Glah was the man pushing the pace. There were six or seven of us at that point, and I thought "This is a lot of company for the Ironman." Usually we're riding with one, two, or three other people. We had seven riders in this loosely knit pack, and I didn't know half of them. That didn't make me feel too secure.

Below: Scott Tinley was two and a half minutes back before we started the seven-mile climb into Hawi. Tinley knew that if we got to the turnaround before him, it would be difficult for him to make up any time on the way back. Tinley caught us right at the turnaround. Notice that even though Tinley appears higher up on his handlebars, he is still in that aerodynamic arrow position where he can cut through the wind.
Photo by Lois Schwartz

a loosely knit bike race. The triathlon drafting rules state that you have to be three feet to the side and two bike lengths behind another cyclist, so people stay six feet to the side and three bike lengths back. In a sense, it's a spread-out pack of bike racers. You're not on each other's wheels, but positions are constantly shifting. People were pulling through, dropping back, and taking the lead.

Suddenly Ken Glah from Westchester, Pennsylvania, caught us. He looked really good, the best I've seen him look in a race. He must have had an awesome swim or a heck of a hard first 40 miles on the bike to join us so quickly. He caught us around Kawaihae, before

After the turnaround in Hawi, we started the ride back to Kona. I'm number 2, and next to me is Keith Anderson (133), Mr. Speedo. Up ahead, out of the saddle, is Scott Tinley (3). Mike Pigg is the other rider in the picture, just ahead of Tinley.
Photo by Lois Schwartz

A triathlon pack reacts the same as a bike-racing pack when someone gets too far off the front. If someone has too big a lead, then one rider has to bridge the gap so the leader doesn't disappear over the horizon. That can be dangerous.

And, remember, the ABC camera vans are out in the lava fields to get the best show they can. If they can get close-ups of sweat rolling off your face, they've got a great show. Unfortunately, it's not too great for the chase group when the truck pulls in tight on the leader, gets a close-up, and creates a little draft. It doesn't have to be long, maybe 15–30 seconds. If the wind is right, a rider can gain 15–30 seconds on the others with just one close-up. This year, the camera van was pretty good about staying on the nonwindy side of the riders. There wasn't as much artifi-

cial assistance from the vans as in the past.

But, with or without the cameras, you can't let anyone get away. I was content to stay with the group. I kept reminding myself that when I got off the bike, I would have to run a marathon. In past races, I've put the run out of my mind. This year, I was acutely aware of what that run would feel like, what I was going to have to do to win the race. Having those thoughts in mind kept me from going maniacal on the bike. I know there were points where I could have gone harder. "No, you don't want to go harder," I thought, "because if you do, you're going to be hating life during the run." I just kept thinking, "Marathon . . . marathon . . . marathon."

When we started hitting the head winds on the way into Hawi, I could tell that Anderson, Mr. Speedo, was having a hard time, because he was pushing too big a gear. At the turnaround, Dave had some problems with his special-needs bag,* and when I looked back, Tinley was no more than two seconds

*Special-needs bag. Ironman contestants can put a favorite food or drink in a bag that can be picked up at the bike turn-around at Hawi.

behind. When we got through the turn, he took off. Everyone was yelling, "Go Dave! Go Dave!" Then all of a sudden, the crowd realized it wasn't Dave—it was Tinley.

To me, the race doesn't start to develop until the way back from Hawi, and now besides Dave Scott, Mike Pigg, and Ken Glah, Scott Tinley, a two-time Ironman winner, had joined us for the ride home. I had a feeling the cat-and-mouse game was about to end. The ride back to Kona would be intense.

Who says the Ironman bike course is flat? Here a few riders take on the Queen Kaahumanu Highway.
Photo courtesy of Bud Light Ironman

Above: The Ironroad, a close-up look at the lovely scenery along the Queen Kaahumanu Highway. Add 100-degree temperatures to the black nothingness of the lava fields, and you'll know why Ironman is not a day in the park.
Photo by C. J. Olivares, Jr.

Below: This is the press caravan that followed the leaders throughout the 1987 Ironman. If you look closely, you can see the ABC van and the leaders. To the right is one of the aid stations located every five miles along the bike ride and every mile along the run.
Photo by Bob Babbitt

In what ways has Ironman changed since 1978? The picture on the left shows Bob Babbitt standing in the transition area of the 1980 Ironman after the swim. He has a $60 bicycle with solid rubber tires and a radio bungee-corded to the handlebars. On the right is the transition area for the 1987 Ironman. The machines the Ironmen ride today cost a little more than $60.

THE TRIATHLON OLYMPICS?

So why is the Ironman such a "heavy" event? Probably because in the eyes of the rest of the world, the Ironman is to triathlon what Xerox is to office copiers and Coca-Cola is to soft drinks. Ironman has become a generic term for the word *triathlon*—but it hasn't happened by accident.

The Ironman was established as a self-proclaimed survival of the fittest. Navy commander John Collins put together the first Ironman in 1978 to settle a long-standing argument: Who really was the toughest? A swimmer, a cyclist, or a runner? To find the answer, Collins combined the 2.4-mile Waikiki rough-water swim, the 112-mile around-Oahu bike ride, and the Honolulu marathon into one full day of pain and suffering. The winner would be the "Ironman," the toughest of the tough. Fourteen crazies participated on Oahu in 1978 and 1979. There were no aid stations back then. To compete, you needed friends or family members who would agree to spend their day driving around Oahu supplying you with food, water, and large doses of encouragement.

In 1979 the event received its first big media boost when *Sports Illustrated* profiled Tom Warren, a tavern owner from San Diego who won the Ironman that year in an upset over defending champion Gordon

Haller. Because of the article, the Ironman began to grow. There were 100 participants in 1980, the last year the race was held on Oahu. When ABC televised the event the same year, its success was signed, sealed, and delivered. Ironman had to move to the big island of Hawaii in 1981 to accommodate the demand. That year 326 triathletes entered, followed by 600 in 1982. According to Rick Gaffney, the press coordinator for the race, Ironman has been filled to capacity every year since.

Ironman also began to establish its international base in 1982. "We started sending press releases all over the world that year," said Gaffney. "Our intention was to raise the level of Ironman's international consciousness." Gaffney was criticized for spending so much money, but it paid off in spades. The number of foreign journalists has now grown to more than 200 representing 41 nations.

Even Xin Hua, mainland China's equivalent to the Associated Press, sends a correspondent to the Ironman each year. "The People's Republic has an open invitation to send an athlete to do the race," said Gaffney, "but they won't until they have someone who can do well." In the meantime, they keep close tabs on the level of competition.

The Iron Curtain countries also have shown an interest in the Ironman. Each year, Gaffney is interviewed by Radio Free Europe to give a postrace synopsis to an estimated 120 million listeners.

During the past few years, Ironman has expanded its international scope by adding to the actual number of Ironman races. In 1988 there will be Ironman-sanctioned triathlons in Japan, Canada, Germany, New Zealand, and, of course, Hawaii. "Eventually, I'm sure there will be an event in Central America, too," said Gaffney.

There obviously is a need for more Iron options. At one point, the Ironman office was receiving ten thousand applications for the Hawaiian event alone. Nowadays, there is a clear process of qualification to become an Ironman participant; very few are accepted through random lottery. If someone wishes to become an Ironman, he or she needs to bring the right credentials to the table. After all, the Ironman is a world-championship event.

According to Gaffney, though, the Ironman is more than that. To him and many others, Ironman is the Olympics of the sport. He has a good point. Athletes participate from 41 nations, there are tough qualifications requirements, an international press corps, plus an American television audience that in 1986 was 6.7 percent of the 86 million homes with television sets. That translates to approximately 5,762,000 households tuned in to the 1986 Ironman.

What started off as a campaign to merely "raise the level of international consciousness" has made the Ironman an incredibly heavy event. Is it heavy enough for an athlete to base a whole career on? It might be. Just ask Dave Scott.

—Bob Babbitt

13
IRONDAY, PART 2

That which you want wants you. That which
you fear finds you.

—Mike Rubano

You can always make it out to Hawi, where you get a little bit of a break. If your body is strong, when you hit the headwind, if you still feel good, you know that you'll have a good bike ride. If you're feeling tired, it's going to be a long way into town from Kawaihae.

Dave was in the lead, followed by Tinley and Pigg. They were riding side by side, and the pack was in a big diamond shape. We were cruising along with the tail wind when Ken Glah went flying by. He got a little antsy and stretched his lead to a minute and a half. Then I noticed that Dave was starting to pull away, and the gap between Dave and Pigg, Tinley, and myself started to get too big for comfort. "Come on, guys," I said to myself, "You'd better stick with him. He's starting to make a move." They didn't go. I thought, "This is it, Grip. Keep him in

range. Stay with his pace."

Once you fall off the pace, even though you feel you're going hard, you slow down. I went by Pigg and Tinley and started hammering. It took me several miles to catch up to Dave, because he was moving along pretty well. I looked back, and Pigg and Tinley hadn't come with me. Right there was the break Dave and I needed to get away from the pack. We caught up to Glah, and I knew he was going too hard. I hadn't ridden ahead of Dave yet, but I thought, "Why pass him? He's riding a pretty good pace. I don't think I want to spoil his fun up there. Why not hang back and cruise on through?"

The wind didn't seem as bad as in the past, and there wasn't a cloud in the sky. Usually as we come back toward town, there's a set of clouds that extend out over the road. They usually appear where the tail wind that

The riders on the left of the photo are on their way out to Hawi. The ones on the right are on their way back. Any way you look at it, you're a long way from town.
Photo by Bob Babbitt

pushes you away from Kawaihae becomes the head wind you battle all the way back to town. The weather was unusual that day.

I kept eating and drinking and listening to what my body needed. I visualized that cathedral arch that I had seen myself gaining strength from before the race. I felt OK through the bike. Somewhere around the airport, I noticed that my back was getting tight off and on. I'd stand up, and it would loosen right up. I felt fine on the uphills, not quite as fatigued as in the past. The wind wasn't bothering me, and I was focusing. Was my pace too fast or too slow? It seemed like the pace I needed to go.

About two miles from town, eight and a half miles before the end of the bike, I went through an aid station and drank some Exceed and some water.

All of a sudden, I felt sick to my stomach. I dropped further behind Dave because I had to slow down and sit up. Without any warning, I threw up everything all at once. Thankfully, the ABC van wasn't in the area. It wasn't very pretty. When you're out on the lava fields, you are what you are. People see the real you.

After I threw up all the food, and the Carbo Plex, I felt much better. But, I knew something wasn't right. That had never happened to me before. I knew I had to ingest some food and liquid because now I was totally empty and couldn't run 26 miles on fumes.

But instead I caught up to Dave, glad that he hadn't seen me lose it. It would only have given him confidence. And even he wouldn't have wanted to see me struggling like that. We rode in together on the bike, climbed up the last hill, and descended into the Kona Surf parking lot. I was feeling pretty good, strong, hydrated, and full of food and energy. In fact, despite everything, I felt better than I ever had at the end of a bike leg. I felt ready to run 26.2 miles.

We came in, and everyone was cheering as we ran into the changing room. I threw on my socks and running shorts and came out of the room ahead of him. He caught me as we started up the hill out to Alii Drive.

Last year at the beginning of the run, all the muscles in my legs felt as if they had fused into one gigantic unit, and it seemed like there was no independent motion of the muscle groups. I felt like I was running with stiff cement legs. This year, I was loose right away. My lower back hurt, but I ignored it.

Dave went flying down the same hill we had crested just minutes before on the bike. I thought, "My God, you're gonna kill yourself running that fast down this hill!" But, as long as the pace was comfortable, I was going to try to stick with him. I don't think Dave has ever started that run without putting time on people, during the first 10K down Alii Drive. I thought, as long as I was running within myself, I was going to try to stay with him. Here we were starting a marathon in the heat of the day. It was at least 100 degrees out, and there was not a cloud in the sky. Any marathoner would tell you you're nuts to do a race under those conditions . . . but that's the Ironman.

As I ran through town, every now and then I thought about how Dave was looking and how he must be feeling.

In spite of throwing up twice during the last 10 miles of the bike ride, I felt better than ever when I got off the bike. Dave Scott (behind me) said later that he felt "weary," that it was the worst he had ever felt after the bike.
Photo by Lois Schwartz

For the most part, I just focused on myself and how I was doing. I imagined my energy dome, the magnetic field. It pumped all my energy back into me. At three and a half miles, Dave fell behind me. I was monitoring my breathing, which was even. I wasn't stressing and I wasn't straining; I wasn't even hot. We were running a moderate pace, and Dave started to fall off. "OK, I can slow down even more and run with him. Who knows? Maybe the guy will cave

My plan was to run with Dave unless he dropped off the pace. The two of us stayed together as we ran through town, but soon my lead grew to 40 seconds as we headed out to the lava fields.

Photo by Lois Schwartz

in on this run. Or, I can run my own race." I decided to just keep it going. I felt good, I felt fine, I wasn't pushing it to any crazy limit. My lead began to grow from 20, then 30, then 43 seconds, and finally to a full minute. I went slow up the hill out of town, which is always a killer hill. It's probably the hottest place on the run course because of the tail wind.

I asked somebody how Dave was looking. He said, "He's not looking bad, but if he was feeling good, he would be right here with you." It was the first time I can think of, other than Ironman 1982 (the year Tinley beat him), that someone had pulled away from Dave on the run.

I went cruising through the aid stations, trying to stay comfortable. I tried to stay aware of my breathing and heart rate—you can't judge how you're doing by speed alone. When the body gets really hot, breathing and heart rate go up, too. You have to maintain a low breathing rate and a low heart rate. Although the effort may not seem hard, if your heart rate and breathing rate are high, you'll blow up. As you start using up fuel in your body, you're running out of glycogen and losing efficiency on burning fat. If you allow the breathing and heart rate to stay high, you're going to run out of gas. You have to back off and slow down.

I got to the turnaround with 10 miles left to go. My game plan before the race had been to go easy enough on the way out that I could run fast the last 10 miles. I've always had great runs in Nice, running the first half easy and the second half hard. To negative-split is the ultimate way to run a race. That's what I wanted to do in Hawaii.

Because there's a tail wind, it gets a

Past 20 miles I could tell that my body wasn't responding to the fluids I was taking in. Earlier, if I drank something, my body felt energized. Now I felt like I had a hole in my gas tank. I decided to stop and walk through an aid station in order to get as much fluid into me as possible. It's easier to drink when you walk than when you run.
Photo by Lois Schwartz

I could feel my heart and breathing rates were starting to climb, plus my body was starting to get too hot. I used the sponges and water at the aid stations to try to keep my body temperature down.
Photo by Lois Schwartz

little hot just before the turn. I started my watch at the turnaround. Dave was four and a half minutes back, and he didn't look good. He was really struggling. I thought, "No reason for me to hammer these last 10 miles, because it *is* 10 miles. I'll just keep the pace I'm going." I felt comfortable, and there was no reason to speed it up.

About one mile past the turnaround, I started to feel like something wasn't right with me. At the next aid station, I decided to eat and drink more than I thought I needed. I thought I'd walk through and take my time to fuel up. I definitely didn't want to bonk on that run.

I went through the aid station and drank Coke, water, and Exceed. But something was out of whack. My body was not responding to what I had put in it. Earlier in the run, water and Exceed had picked me up right away. Now, there was no response. After the aid station, I had to really slow my pace down. I was starting to run out of gas. I walked through the next aid station, but still no response. I thought, "Just stay focused, stay relaxed; you don't know what is going on behind you. If you have to slow down and start walking, you're going to have to start walking. That's all there is to it. If Dave beats you, he beats you. If you beat him, that's fine. If you end up 10th, that's what's going to happen. Nothing can be done at this point."

Between that aid station and the next one, my body shut down. It wasn't absorbing anything. During that last little stretch of running, my breathing rate was going up. My body wasn't working the way it had been. I wasn't hot or dehydrated. I told myself, "Don't give up. You can respond, you can come around."

I picked it up again and made it to the next aid station, where I ate and drank. It still didn't help. My body just wasn't absorbing energy. It felt like the food and water were going through the system but my body wasn't taking it in. There was a tightness in my stomach and intestines. It felt like I had to go to the bathroom, but whenever I tried, nothing would happen. At this point it was turning into a walk, jog, walk, jog. This isn't the way you want to run your marathon.

It was pointless to look back to see if Dave was coming. If he was, there was nothing I could do. Looking back wasn't going to make me go any faster. I was doing all I could. I heard reports that he was 2½ minutes behind, then 30 seconds. "OK," I said to myself, "He'll be coming along any minute."

He passed me on the right side of the road. I was walking when he went by. It was ludicrous to think that I could rally and go with him. I was doing all I could do.

My body continued to ignore the food and liquid I put in it. Finally, I was forced to a walk.
Photo by Lois Schwartz

I thought, "Unless he falls apart, he's got the race. Just don't give up. Do what you can do, walk as little as you have to, and run as much as you can. Who knows? You may be able to finish second. You may pass Dave; he may slow down. A few miles ago, he probably thought the race was over and I was going to win. There's always a chance."

It was then that things got bad. At

. . . And here's Keith Anderson, wearing the original no-frills triathlon outfit—Speedo, shades, and visor.
Photo by Lois Schwartz

one point I went to the bathroom and realized I was bleeding inside. It scared me. What had I done? The time between aid stations was like an eternity, and I struggled from one eternity to the next.

When I passed Julie coming the other way, she was walking with two cups of ice water in her hands. That was when I was really struggling. We walked together for a while. "How far back did he pass you?" she asked. "Oh, not even a half-mile ago," I said. I could see the disappointment on her face. It's exciting to be in the lead and to see friends when everything is going the

When things start to go bad, you try to make do with what you've got. If my body was functioning at only 20 percent of capacity, it was important to me to get 100 percent out of that 20 percent. But, as you can tell, I wasn't real excited about this situation. I knew that soon I was going to face my biggest fear, that someone was going to pass me during the run.
Photo by Lois Schwartz

I had a few fears before I went to Hawaii. One was swimming more than a half-mile offshore during those days before the race. The big fish swim out there, right? Another fear was having a big lead and watching it disappear without being able to do anything about it. This photo was taken not long before Dave Scott caught me and forced me to face that fear.
Photo by Lois Schwartz

way it should. It's hard to disappoint them when it's not.

The last little hill into town was like climbing Mount Everest. The marshall who was next to me said, "Just get up this hill, come on, you've got it made!" I got to the top, and down the other side. I was walking and running again. I was surprised no one else caught up to me. It seemed like those last four miles since Dave went by took a long, long, time. I ran the last few hundred yards and tried to wave to the crowd. Hearing their cheers as I came in filled me up with emotion.

I'm sure a lot of people thought the race was over when I was four and a half minutes ahead and still gaining. But that's the Ironman. Things change out there. I gave 100 percent of whatever I had. At the end, I was probably running on 20 percent of my potential, and I squeezed 100 percent out of that. I crossed the line and gave thanks that I was alive, that I was still in second place.

At that point, I didn't care whether or not I had won the race. I had gone from racing to having to walk and run. All I wanted to do was get across the line and have people check out my body and make sure I was OK.

It puts things in a totally different perspective when your body falls apart on you. I didn't care that I lost to Dave Scott, or anyone else for that matter. "He can have the damn thing this year!" I just wanted to know that I was OK and that my body would be at 100 percent at some point again.

Sure, I was disappointed. It was disappointing to feel things fall apart and not have the race go the way I wanted. But to get 100 percent out of any situation is all any of us can ask for.

14
REACHING THE
LOW OF LOWS

Maturity is not succeeding all the time.
Maturity is continuing to try even when we
are failing.

—David K. Reynolds

When I crossed the finish line, I really felt bad. The race officials took me into the medical tent, lay me down, and started an IV on me. My father was there, and I could see the concern on his face. My mom and my brother were there, too. The only thing I was thinking was, "Dave, you can have this whole thing, you can win it as many times as you want, it's not worth it." There are other races, other challenges. This one, the Ironman, can be so absolutely taxing on the body, I wonder if I'm totally insane to keep coming back.

I've only had two Ironman finishes where I didn't have to walk. In five tries, I've never raced the event the way I wanted to. Lying in the medical tent after Ironman '87, I asked myself, "How many times are you going to keep doing this, especially when you're lying here and your stomach and intestines are wrapped around each other?"

When I went to the bathroom, it was obvious that I was still bleeding internally. I asked my dad, "What do they do for something like this?" He said, "All they can do is keep filling you full of fluids so you don't get dehydrated from blood loss."

They finally took me from the medical tent to the hospital in an ambulance. I almost got there without throwing up. I lost it in the hospital driveway. When I got to the emergency room, the doctors stuck a tube down my nose, back down my throat, and into my stomach. They pumped cold water in and out, which helped to stop the bleeding. Then they checked my body temperature, and woke me every few hours to get a blood sample and take my blood pressure. All night long, I felt as if someone was punching me in the stomach.

My four-and-a-half-minute lead had totally disappeared in a matter of six miles. Dave Scott went on to win his sixth Ironman Triathlon.
Photo by Lois Schwartz

I had to be content with second place. I also received an all-expenses-paid trip to the medical tent followed by an evening in one of the Big Island's finest hospitals.
Photo by Lois Schwartz

I had reached the low of lows. First I started bleeding out of my nose. Then I threw up during the bike ride and started to bleed internally during the run. I ended the day in the hospital with some nurse sticking a thermometer up my ass. If racing the Ironman was like birth, I had this sneaking suspicion I'd been born breech. I continually had to remind myself that there was a reason for all this, that this was the way it was supposed to happen.

I woke up the next morning and, like 1,500 other triathletes, I was faced with reality. The Ironman was over. I had put a lot of time and energy into it and had high expectations. No matter what happened, each of us was faced with our performance, and we were going to have to live with it. For some it would be easy, because they did great. Others had absolutely no expectations and did better than they ever could have imagined.

Another group woke up to a different reality. They didn't perform to their expectations. They had to wake up and live with it. No more hiding behind, "Well, I know I'm going to have a good performance, because I've done the training," or, "I know I can push through the pain because I've had great workouts." No more conjecture, only fact and reality. How you relate to that is the ultimate test. It's not how you did in the race, it's how you *relate* to how you did that will carry you through and provide you with new strength.

Ironman gives you a different reference point. My performance didn't turn out the way I wanted it to, but it gave me a total strength that I didn't have before. When you do shorter races, you're not always tested to the fullest. You're not faced with as many moments of inner truth. At Ironman, you willingly put yourself through what can be a completely agonizing test. All of a sudden, when you're done, other things don't sound so difficult. The race helps to stabilize you.

Because of the condition I finished in, Ironman gave me an additional lifetime of wisdom. That performance is symbolic of how things can go in life. It was a tough race, my body was falling apart on me, but somehow I made it through.

I'm not really sure what happened to me that day. I'm still wrestling with it. I guess it was an exercise-induced body destruction of sorts. And an intestinal virus helped it on its way. Of all the days to get the flu bug, Ironday isn't one of them.

I woke up to a few other realities the morning after the race. One was the reality of tubes sticking in my body. Another was Dave Scott's anger. The nurse brought me the newspaper, and the first thing I read was how Dave was upset because I was on his feet during the swim. I thought, "My God, here he wins the damn race, and he's whining because someone was on his feet during the swim!" After such an intense race, your body is charged with emotion and taxed completely. It's been through a couple hours of discomfort, several more of difficulty and pain, and then two or three of sheer physical torture. The body wants to just stop, but your mind keeps telling it to go. There is a point where each step can seem to pull you toward this vast yet painful area we call our unknown limit.

Dave felt frustration because it was a hard race. He wasn't the main attraction in Hawaii, like he had been in the past. It was like coming home after a hard day at work and expecting the family to cater to him. When he got home, when he arrived in Hawaii, someone else was in his house getting all his attention. That someone else was me.

Dave had to deal with seeing his race and domain slipping away from him, and the pain it took to bring it back into his grasp. I had to see my best-laid plans go from a dream to a reality, and then see them slipping back into the hands of the man who dealt the last harsh blows to his challengers on the Kona Coast.

After the turnaround every challenger you pass provides the moment-to-moment support you need to get you to the finish line. But your ultimate goal to win depends on who's in front of you. That intensity often becomes difficult to release after the race is finished.

It's one thing when someone pushes you in a race but you're able to maintain control. In 1986, I had a great, great race. I felt Dave was thankful that I was out there. My presence was one factor that helped him to have a good race, too. In 1987 he felt it was the Mark Allen Show. He wasn't comfortable. He wasn't getting enough water on the run, and he started to fall off the pace. He was pushed beyond the point where he was in control of his own race.

There are comfort zones within your zone of discomfort. Then there is a discomfort zone within the discomfort zone. That's when you say, "It's too much. I wish you weren't here. I don't like being in this much pain." I think Dave went deep into his discomfort zone that year.

I know I've felt that way in workouts, when someone is pushing me beyond the limits and way beyond a great workout. If you're forced to dig down into your reserves, you get pissed off. I felt that way after the last Golden Gate Canyon ride with Souza and Pigg. I had to dig a little too deep. I was upset because we went too hard.

A race like the Ironman is the equivalent of two heavyweights going 15 rounds beating the hell out of each other. It takes a while for the pain to subside and to get the emotion of the race out of your system before you can see and respect another's performance. Sometimes after an experience like that, you are forced to look hard at the dark side of yourself. Unfortunately, you might not like what you see.

15
EPILOGUE

*Swallowing error or accomplishment of the
recent past, we turn to the next moment,
always a fresh one, always carrying with it the
possibility of new achievement.*
                                    —David K. Reynolds

Will I ever do Ironman again? My body still needs time to recover. It's funny. Right after the race, I never wanted to do that race again. People who want it can have it. They can go out there, thrash themselves, and get all the glory. I was on the Big Island a couple of days after the race, and just driving down Alii Drive practically made me sick. For weeks, I couldn't eat without getting nauseated. I suppose it will take time for me to forget the negatives of the day.

Ironman is a big event, not so much in importance, but in what you go through during such a short period of time. You have to constantly remind yourself of the equality of all things, especially when you let the importance of one race become so outrageous and so big it puts you out of balance and reduces your ability to see things clearly

in your life. To get back on track, you need to release yourself from the emotions that can bind you hopelessly to that race's outcome. You have to be able to learn and grow from the competition.

Unless you test yourself, you stagnate. Unless you try to go way beyond what you've been able to do before, you won't develop and grow. When you test yourself beyond your usual limit, when you go for it 100 percent, when you don't have that fear of "what if I fail," that's when you learn, that's when you are really living.

You're also really living if you face your fears. One of my ultimate fears before the Ironman was that I was going to fall apart during the run. I thought about being in the lead and having someone come by me. When Dave did go by, I said to myself, "Face your fear. It's happening." When you

What does the future hold for Mark Allen? Maybe I'll get a grip on life after triathlons as a T.V. color analyst. At the Catalina Triathlon in November 1987, I interviewed many of the top triathletes for a television special. Andrew McNaughton, who gave me such a hard time at the 1987 President's Triathlon, is the interviewee.
Photo by Bob Babbitt

avoid a fear, when you're staring at it face-to-face and you run away, it gets bigger. "Face your fear," I said at the time. "Keep going and no one else will pass you."

The more of those situations you are aware of and face, the closer you get to the spot I call the center, your energy spot. For me, there is a point where I can stand and nothing can knock me off. To find yours, face your fears, and acknowledge that they are there.

If I am centered, if I have reached my energy spot, I should be able to just sit in a corner by myself and be happy. As an athlete, I sometimes imagine that I'm in a crowd of world-class athletes receiving awards for excellence. As the awards are presented, everyone claps. All the athletes in the room receive an award but me, even though I had a fantastic season. I'd be in my ultimate place within myself; I would be in my energy spot if, after not receiving an award, I could feel sincerely happy for everyone else. If I knew myself what I had accomplished, that it was the best I could do, the praise wouldn't have to come from an external source. I should be happy with myself.

I'll be the first to admit it: I'm not there yet. But I'm getting closer!

APPENDIX 1
MARK ALLEN'S
TRAINING SCHEDULE

Here is my training schedule, beginning with the early-season training (January–March), leading into the midseason (April–July), and ending in the late season (August–October). As I've said before, you should train according to the routine that works best for you. Hopefully, my workout schedule will give you some tips that will help you out with your own training.

TRAINING SCHEDULE

	Swim (yards)	Bike (miles)	Run (miles)
Early Season			
Monday	3,300	70	—
Tuesday	3,700	40	10
Wednesday	—	55	8
Thursday	3,400	—	10
Friday	3,800	50	—
Saturday	—	75	9
Sunday	—	—	15
Total	14,200	290	52

TRAINING SCHEDULE

	Swim (yards)	Bike (miles)	Run (miles)
Midseason			
Monday	4,100	70	8
Tuesday	3,600	50	13
Wednesday	—	80	5
Thursday	4,500	—	5
Friday	3,900	40	10
Saturday	—	85	—
Sunday	2,000 easy	25	18
Total	18,100	350	59
Late Season			
Monday	4,300	60	9
Tuesday	—	120	5
Wednesday	4,800	40	14
Thursday	4,100	70	7
Friday	3,900	90	10
Saturday	—	112	—
Sunday	3,000	—	22
Total	20,100	492	67

Stationary Bike Workout

10-minute warm-up

Gearing	Duration
52 × 19	Approximately 100 rpm for 5 minutes
52 × 18	Same
52 × 17	Same
52 × 15	Same
52 × 14	Same
52 × 13	Same
42 × 17	10 minutes, spin easy, both legs
42 × 15	20 minutes, left leg, gear should be hard enough so you use muscle through entire stroke
42 × 17	5 minutes, both legs
42 × 15	20 minutes, right leg
42 × 17	5 minutes, both legs

Repeat 4 times:

42 × 17	15 seconds, fast spin, all out
42 × 17	45 seconds, easy

Total Workout: 1½ hours 1 to 2 times a month

──────────── **Special Types of Road Speed Work** ────────────

1. A 10- to 12-mile time trial: record your time each week

2. Undulating hill sprints on a 20 mile course (approximately 18–20 individual sprints, hard on uphills, easy on downhills

3. During a 20–30 mile group ride take turns pulling for 20 seconds. Use big gear (52 × 15) while pulling and small gear (42 × 15 or 17) while sitting in.

──────────── **Track Workouts** ────────────

Sample workouts for a nonrace week:

Always do 2½–5 miles of actual fast running. This means the total workout with warm-up and cool-down will be about 10 miles.

Warm-up 2 miles easy	
Stretch	
6 × 100 m	Moderate, jog back
5 × 1,000 m	Descend time for each one, 400 m jog in between
4 × 400 m	Fast, 100–400 m jog
2 miles	Loosen-down, stretch
Total:	4–5 miles, fast

Warm-up 2 miles easy	
Stretch	
1 mile	Straights fast, turns slow, get faster as you go
2 × 440	
880	
1,320	
1,320	100–400 m jog in between
880	
2 × 440	
6 × 100 m	Grass striding
2 miles	Loosen down, easy stretch
Total:	4–5 miles, fast

Warm-up 2 miles easy	
Stretch	
10 × 100	Moderate
10 × 400	First 5: 400 jog in between
	Second 5: 100 jog in between, with second 5 as fast as the last 400 of the first 5
1 mile	Loosen down
10 × 100	Strides on grass
2 miles	Loosen down, stretch
Total:	Approximately 4 miles, fast

─────────────────── **Workout for Race Week** ───────────────────

Warm-up 2.5 miles		
	10 × 100	Strides on grass
	3 × 400	Straights moderately hard, curves very easy, 400 jog in between
	¾ mile	Easy
	8 × 100	Strides
	1 mile	Easy, stretch
	Total:	Approximately 3 km, fast

I prefer doing sets of 1,000 meters and miles with straights and curves. For triathlons, those give you the best combination of strength and speed. You need the 400s to really open up the legs, but 1,000s seem to help build speed and strength at the same time.

APPENDIX 2
MONITORING
YOUR TRAINING

I've talked a lot about training, about listening to my body, about using a heart monitor. I know it sounds regimented. On one hand, if you keep everything under control and don't overdo it, you won't get injured and you'll do great in the races. On the other hand, there will be times where you need to throw everything aside and just go for it. Sometimes, even when you're tired, go as hard as you can go and really thrash yourself.

Training is not an absolute science. Look at the top guys. We all train differently. I lean toward harder workouts rather than longer workouts, but Tinley and Molina do longer mileage. Their consistency gives them strength for the races. Dave will have periods when he can train well and others when he can't. Pigg is a good example of a guy who goes by the book, but I know firsthand that a lot of times he'll

go out there and thrash himself just to see what his body can take.

This summer Pigg packed up and drove nonstop from Arcata, California, to Boulder, Colorado. He arrived in town at 3:30 in the morning and he'd had maybe two hours of sleep. Souza, Molina, and I were getting up to do a really long run that morning. Then Pigg called. With two hours of sleep, he was ready for a full-on major run up a route called the Switzerland Trail. It starts at 8,000 feet, climbs to 9,500 feet, drops down, and then goes back up again. I had had my full 10 hours of sleep and was wondering if *I* was going to run. Pigg finished the run and taught us all that you don't have to be fresh to have a great workout. Sometimes you just push yourself and do it.

When it comes to performance and doing well in a race, there is no shortcut to putting in the miles, to building a base. You start by getting in shape each year, then add speed work. Finally it's time for a little early-season race experience. There are some shortcuts through visualization and creating positive images. But training smart is the common thread that links successful training programs.

I didn't train smart when I started out. For 11 years before the triathlon, I was a competitive swimmer. When you swim, basically every workout is hard. You go as hard as you can every time you get into the pool.

I tried to carry this philosophy into running and cycling. I didn't have a running or cycling coach, so I made a few mistakes that slowed down my progress. I spent my first couple of years in triathlon getting injured periodically during my training, especially from running, You name the running injury, and I had it. But in the process of adapting my body and mentality to what it would take to run and cycle well, I learned how to push myself and go hard in those two sports. The tendons, joints, and ligaments aren't meant to go 100 percent every time you run or bike. If you go as hard as you can every time out, you'll be injured before you do your first race. Your body needs a period of time to recover from the day-to-day pounding.

In swimming, I already knew how to go hard. If you're a weak swimmer, you need to get in a program where someone is on the deck working on your stroke mechanics. A coach will psych you up and push you to your limits.

The best way to improve performance in swimming is to improve the flexibility in your shoulders and to work on your stroke. Marathon runner Rob de Castella could not beat an eight- or ten-year-old national-caliber swimmer. De Castella is in better shape, but his stroke is less efficient and in turn counterproductive. My suggestion is to get in a Masters program where someone is available to coach you and help with your stroke mechanics.

At first, I tried to adapt my swim program, which was all anaerobic, to running and cycling. Because I was injured all the time, I didn't do long mileage those first couple of years. I went 200 miles a week on the bike, and I was lucky if I got my running mileage up to 40. That wasn't much compared to Tinley's or Molina's mileage at the time.

My intensity was always high when I was doing the shorter mileage. I was lifeguarding at the time, so I had to ride my bike before work. Invariably, I'd be ten miles from work and only have time to go five. I'd ride as hard as I could and try to make up the time so I wouldn't be late. This was my daily speed workout on the bike. I had a fair amount of success with that. I learned that you can do a few races really well on short, intense interval training. However, your recovery won't be as fast as for someone who puts in longer mileage and does over-distance work. Consequently, you won't be able to do as many races as someone who has more time to train and has put in those longer miles.

The more experienced I became, the more I realized it takes a couple of years to build a running and cycling base to strengthen the joints and ligaments to a point where they can take the pounding and the stress. Remember, when you're training, muscles develop faster than joints and liga-

Training on hills can help make racing on them a little easier.
Photo by Lois Schwartz

long moderate run should average 7½–8 minutes per mile. Don't go at high intensity all the time.

If you're doing your workouts right, you'll build both an aerobic base and an anaerobic threshold. By training at a fast pace for a short period of time, you can tolerate that same pace for a longer period, come race day. That's what you get from speed work. An increased ability to be efficient comes from moderate and steady training. To do that, you don't need to go hard. In fact, if you go hard and go into oxygen debt, you don't really work on your ability to increase aerobic capacity.

I started training with a heart moni-

When Scott Tinley first started in triathlons, he was very lean, almost skinny, because he was primarily a runner. As you can tell, weight work and years of training in the pool have helped to build up his upper body.
Photo by Lois Schwartz

ments. You need to keep that in mind when you're building your program.

I couldn't figure out why Tinley and Molina could work out at a slower pace and still beat me. What were they doing that I wasn't? Eventually, I learned that you don't need to run fast during every workout to run fast in a race. In fact it is almost the opposite. You do need to do key speed workouts, but you don't need to do them all the time, every day. Your body will have time to recover when you work out at a slower pace. If your speed work consists of workouts at a 5-minute pace on the track, your

The triathlon is known as a high-tech sport. Here Bill Leach (right), one of the top 40-year-old triathletes, and fellow pro Mark Montgomery ride the Scott DH handlebars. Notice how aerodynamic the body becomes when the elbows are in tight. With the hands close together, the body is in the form of an arrow and actually pierces the wind.
Photo by Lois Schwartz

tor so that I could separate my workouts into an aerobic and an anaerobic system. Basically, an aerobic workout is one in which I train my body to burn fats by running for at least 1½ hours or riding for at least 2½ hours. In an anaerobic workout, such as a hard interval session at the track, I train my body to burn glucose. Your body, given a choice, will develop the glucose system because it's easier to make those enzymes. It's more difficult to turn your body on to developing the fat-burning process.

What I've done the last few years is divide my season into aerobic and anaerobic workouts. In January, February, and March, I do purely aerobic work. I add the speed work, the anaerobic workouts, around mid or late March, so that I have three, four, or five weeks of speed work before my first race. I carry that through for 8–12 weeks. Sometime during the middle of the season, I'll go back to aerobic work for one, two, or three weeks, depending on how my schedule works. At the end of the season, I'll switch back to speed work.

To find your aerobic and anaerobic thresholds, find your training heart rate. Take 220, subtract your age, and that's your maximum heart rate. Eighty percent of that should give you the highest heart rate at which you'll still be aerobic. For me, I take 220 − 29 which is 191. Eighty percent of that equals 153. If I train at 153 heartbeats or less, I'm maintaining an aerobic pace, whether I'm running, cycling, or swimming. When I have my heart monitor on, I try to train within 10 beats of my aerobic maximum of 153 when I'm on a long, fat-burning workout. I try to maintain my heart rate between 143 and 153 the entire period of the workout and never go over that. If I do, I switch into glucose burning, and my body doesn't develop the aerobic fat-burning system.

Here's an example of how I use my heart monitor in my training. One day I went to the track and did a five-mile time trial—not for speed, but for heart rate. I saw how fast I ran for five miles maintaining that heart rate of 153 beats per minute. When I first started doing this workout, my average pace for those five miles at 153 heartbeats per minute was somewhere around 6:45. If I had gone faster—say, a 6:30 pace—my heart rate would have been elevated to 160–162. Then I would have been anaerobic.

As your body becomes more and more efficient, as you develop the enzymes to burn the fat, you will increase your aerobic capacity. Eventually you'll be able to run at a faster pace while maintaining the same heart rate. After training with my monitor for six months, I went back to the track again. This time, instead of 6:45 pace for five miles at 153 heartbeats per minute, I was somewhere around 5:55 per mile. I was running almost one minute per mile faster than before and maintaining the same heart rate. If you train this way, you should go faster in a race than before. If you go head-to-head with someone who hasn't done the same pace building you have he's going to be more anaerobic than you are. That means you are still burning a higher level of fat than he is at any given pace. In an endurance event, you want to burn as much fat as you can. Hopefully, through this type of training, you will have more glucose left over to burn during that final sprint than your opponent. It's important to train your body to learn how to burn fats if you plan to compete in events that take longer than an hour.

Marathon runners have been training this way for a long time, so they are able to stay aerobic when they're running a 5:00 pace. They're just starting to tap into that anaerobic glucose-burning phase when the pace dips to 4:50 per mile.

SAMPLE HEART-MONITOR WORKOUTS

I've included here a full week of heart-monitor workouts from 41-year-old Gary Hooker of Leucadia, California. Hooker held the 40–44-year-old age division record (10:19) at the Ironman for five years, plus he won his division in Ironman twice. He also ran a 4:10 1,500 meter when he was 42 years old. Hooker, along with his partner, Ron Smith, have established a company called Monitor, which makes and markets a computer-enhanced endurance-training system that is heart-monitor based, geared toward the athlete who has less than 20 hours a week to train. Hooker feels that if the training is done right, there is no reason to put in more than 15 hours per week. His system uses a CIC Heartwatch which constantly records your heart rate, and a computer interface which is used to graph your entire training heart rate. The idea is to record each workout and then, using the computer, keep track of all the specifics.

PULSE RATE CURVE

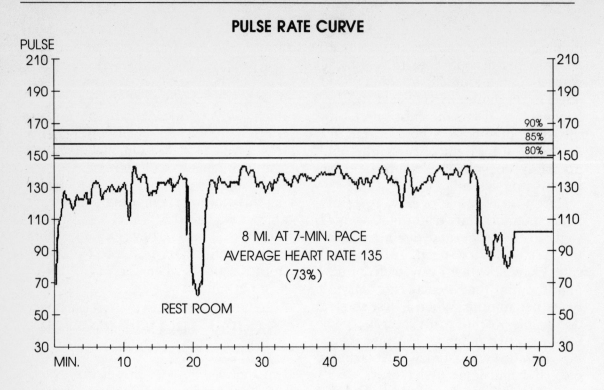

8 MI. AT 7-MIN. PACE
AVERAGE HEART RATE 135
(73%)

REST ROOM

Monday Morning

On Monday, Gary ran an eight-miler at a seven-minute pace. This is a recovery run after a 20-miler on Sunday. With his heart rate at an average of 135 beats per minute, he was running at 73 percent of his maximum heart rate of 185. Gary believes the formula of 220 minus your age can vary in reliability between 10 and 20 beats per minute. As an example, Gary's maximum heart rate should be 174 according to the formula; from testing, he's found that it is actually 185.

PULSE RATE CURVE

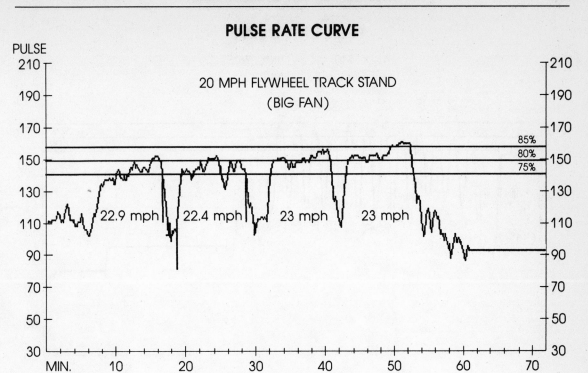

Monday Afternoon

Gary kept his heart rate between 75 percent and 85 percent during 4 10-minute intervals on the stationary bike. He kept his speed right around 23 miles per hour the entire time. Notice that his heart rate became higher as the workout continued. I would call this a fast tempo workout. During the winter months (when this was done), Gary's emphasis is his running. But while he's doing that, he's maintaining his cycling base.

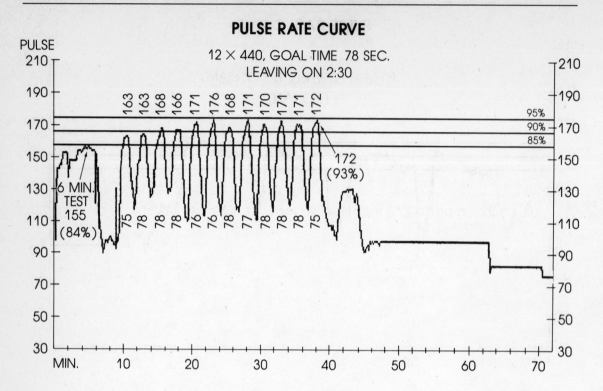

PULSE RATE CURVE

12 × 440, GOAL TIME 78 SEC.
LEAVING ON 2:30

Tuesday

On Tuesday, Gary started off with the six-minute test. He ran a six-minute mile and recorded his heart rate at the end. He does an evenly paced six-minute mile before every quality anaerobic workout. From the results, he can monitor how he's feeling, if he's overtrained or overtired. He did the six-minute test at 155 beats per minute, which is 84 percent of his maximum heart rate of 185. If his heart rate went up to 90 percent, he would know something was wrong and possibly modify the workout. At 80 percent, he'd be in peak condition, ready to race. He followed the six-minute test with 12 × 440. He tried to do each 440 repeat in around 78 seconds, and he started every 2:30.

PULSE RATE CURVE

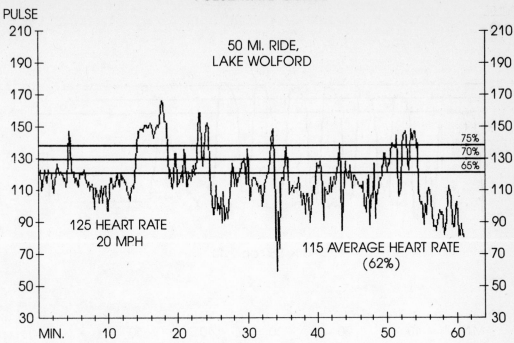

50 MI. RIDE,
LAKE WOLFORD

125 HEART RATE
20 MPH

115 AVERAGE HEART RATE
(62%)

Wednesday

On Wednesday, Gary did a 50-mile fat-burning ride. His average heart rate was 115 beats per minute, which is 62 percent of his maximum. This is not an all-out effort, but a moderate ride with friends. Notice the difference between riding on roads and indoors. Inside, without stoplights and cars, it's easier to be consistent throughout the workout. It's not quite as much fun, though, as riding with a group.

PULSE RATE CURVE

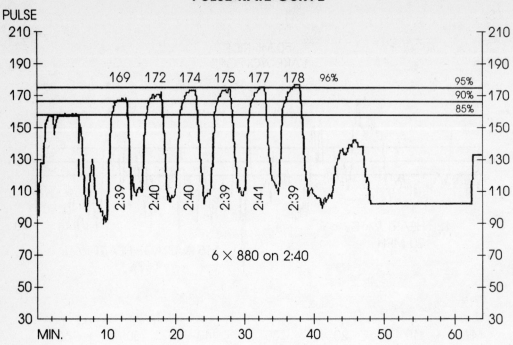

Thursday

Gary starts out with the six-minute test again. Notice that his heart rate is up to 158, over the 155 from earlier in the week. Obviously, he's a little more tired. This time the workout is 6 × 880. When you run intervals, the idea is to maintain form and to leave feeling like you could have done one more.

The same way a weight lifter would not start a workout with a heavy weight, you don't want to start your interval day running too hard. By the end of the session, Gary is up to a heart rate of 178, which is 96 percent of his maximum heart rate. Anything over 95 percent is called no-man's land. You really open yourself up to injury when you go that hard.

PULSE RATE CURVE

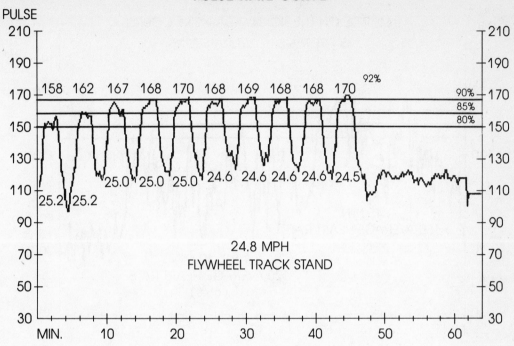

Friday

Gary again brought the bike indoors for a series of 10 one-mile repeats. You can do this workout on a measured road course. He tried to maintain the same speed throughout the workout, but when his heart rate started getting up to 170 halfway through, he adjusted the workout and cut back his speed just a bit to stay under 90 percent of his maximum heart rate. Notice his speed was faster than on Monday. This is more of an anaerobic workout to maintain speed.

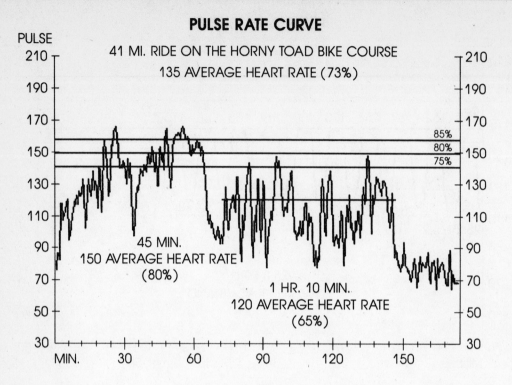

PULSE RATE CURVE

41 MI. RIDE ON THE HORNY TOAD BIKE COURSE
135 AVERAGE HEART RATE (73%)

Saturday

Gary did a 41-mile ride. He went out hard during the first half, took a break, then decided to come back easy.

PULSE RATE CURVE

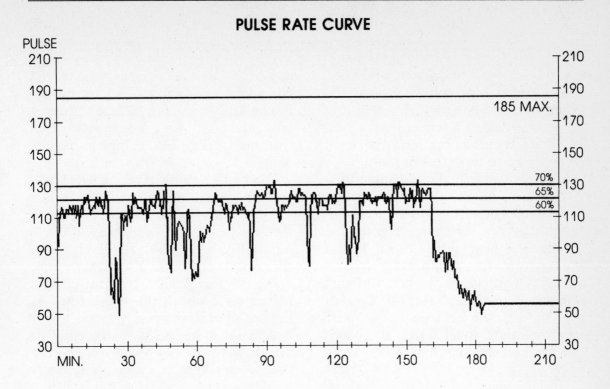

Sunday

On Sunday, Gary did a 20-mile fat-burning run at basically an eight-minute pace. He never went faster than 7:30 per mile. He calls that 2-miler his sightseeing run, because he checks out the new construction along the way. The idea of the fat-burner is just to put in the miles, to be out there for two hours. Without the ability to burn fats, the body tends to run out of fuel, or glycogen, on race day.

Knowing your heart rate can save you from overtraining on days when you're tired, when your body is weak. If your heart rate escalates too easily, your heart may be telling you to rest. When you're just starting a training program, it takes a while, maybe two or three months, for your pace to come down to an efficient point.

A lot of people make the same mistake I did: they work out too hard. Their bodies don't learn to burn fat, because they are constantly training at too high a heart rate. When I first started training with a heart monitor, I felt I was going too slow when my heart rate was between 150 and 160. It takes a period of time before you get more efficient—then you'll burn fat, absorb oxygen, and start running and cycling faster.

I use the heart monitor when cycling, too. I either ride at a moderate pace or I ride hard. During the building phase, I'm into the moderate mode. Then, as I get closer to the season, I go quite a bit harder.

During the anaerobic phase, when I'm doing speed work, when I time-trial on the bike, I want to maintain a heart rate well above that aerobic-anaerobic threshold point. I'll go out and do a 10-mile time trial and see how high I can hold my heart rate. I constantly watch my heart rate to get a feel for what I can maintain for 10 miles. Let's say I can maintain a pace of 166 beats per minute. Now, I know I can get my heart rate higher than that, maybe up to 170, 172. But I can maintain that for only 30 seconds or a minute, and then I have to drop back down because it's too hard.

I'll also do interval work to increase my heart rate's high end. On the bike I'll go for one minute hard and one minute easy. Then two minutes hard, two minutes easy. When I'm going hard, I try to get my heart rate as high as I can. It's not necessarily something I can maintain for very long, but what I'm looking to do is to push my anaerobic threshold. If I go beyond that threshold, I'll go into complete oxygen debt.

I'll do the same type of workouts when I'm running on the track. When you're doing mile repeats, because they're so long, you're only able to maintain that threshold level for a short period of time. But when you're doing 880s or 1,000s, you can go at a higher level almost the entire time. At the end of each interval, you want your heart rate up high. That will push your anaerobic threshold up even higher, so that when you're in a race going really hard, you'll have a higher top end than you would if you hadn't done those workouts.

When you do a time trial or an interval session, you're getting a feel for being at a pace you can maintain when you're going very, very hard. You know what that top end feels like, when you're squeezing every single ounce of oxygen and muscle tissue to its max, to that blackout limit you can't go beyond. In a race, you'll know where those limits are, what they feel like. Obviously, a race brings out more than you could ever get out of a workout. This kind of training shows you what it's like to go that hard, when you reach that peak efficiency level.

Even with a great program, sometimes you'll be doing everything by the book and still have a sneaking suspicion that you're never going to improve. Stick with it. What you've reached is called a plateau. A plateau is a point

The best part of training for and racing in a triathlon is usually when the race is over. From left to right, Joy Hansen, George Hoover, Julie Moss, and I relax after the Kauai Triathlon in 1985.
Photo by C. J. Olivares, Jr.

where you think you're not improving. In reality, your body is learning how to work at a more efficient level. All of a sudden, the body will move to the next level of efficiency. When I reach a plateau, I know improvement is just around the corner.

When I was a kid, I saw the Olympics on TV and decided to go out for the swim team. At the time, I couldn't even swim a lap. I remember that to get into the diving section of the pool, you had to be able to swim 25 yards across it. You'd think this would be no big deal, but it was.

One day I was playing in the diving area, and I must have looked like I couldn't swim very well, because the lifeguard said, "Excuse me, we have to make sure you can swim 25 yards." "OK," I said. I went over and jumped off the edge. It seemed like it took forever to get to the other end. I had to rest there for five minutes before I could pull myself out of the pool. Then it took another five minutes to recover enough to jump off the diving board.

My swimming career started from ground zero. After my diving pool episode, I went for a tryout with the swim team. This was the last time I remember barely being able to swim 25 yards. The next thing I knew, I was able to go 100 yards and could do it a couple of times in a row. I amazed myself with what I was able to do.

When you start out, progress comes quickly. Then you reach a plateau, that hard spot where mentally you don't have the motivation of constantly improving times. But you have to be realistic. Every time you go out, you're not going to do your best time on the track, or in a time trial on the bike. But you're building a base, and it all helps out—you're building knowledge of what your body can do. That knowledge, however, doesn't always stick with you.

In San Diego, we have a ride called the New Year's Day Hangover 100. We meet bright and early New Year's Day at 8:00 and go for a 100-mile ride—not exactly the easiest task after some of the New Year's Eves many of us have had. But it's exciting to start the new year on the bike.

The year I went to Cyprus for the Superstar competition, I hadn't been on the bike for a couple of months. When it came time for the Hangover 100, I thought, "I've been doing this sport for a couple of years, I've put in my time on my bike. I can make 100 miles no matter what, no matter how slow I go." I started out feeling great. You know how the first workout of the year feels,

right? It feels wonderful after not doing it for a couple of months. I cruised the first 40 miles, and it was easy. At 50 miles, all of a sudden, things were getting a little tough. It's an out-and-back course, so when you get to 50 miles, you have no options, there is only one way back, and it's 50 more miles. At 80 miles, my tongue was hanging on the ground and getting caught in the spokes. At 90 I had to stop and get a pillow so I could take a nap on the handlebars. I bonked the last 10 miles so bad, I couldn't even draft off people.

I learned a New Year's lesson. You have to be consistent in your training. It's OK to put on that winter layer of fat and to take time off. The body needs a reserve so then when you get into training again, you're rested and strong. The fatigue of overtraining catches up with you. In swimming I overtrained for too many years and now it's the hardest of the three sports for me to do. Don't ever let yourself get to that point. If you're going to be your own hero, you don't want to be a burned-out hero. No one likes a toasted triathlete.

INDEX